To the wonderful pec [barcode: D0979483]

Thank you for your supp[...] ... [...]
work among the Wanerige in Burkina
Faso. May this book give you more
tools to continue to help more
missionaries.

Till All have heard,
Blaine + Michelle Warner

Beyond Ourselves

HOW CAN THE UNREACHED BE REACHED?

D. Kroeker

WESTBOW
PRESS
A DIVISION OF THOMAS NELSON
& ZONDERVAN

WestBow Press books may be ordered through booksellers or by contacting:

WestBow Press
A Division of Thomas Nelson & Zondervan
1663 Liberty Drive
Bloomington, IN 47403
www.westbowpress.com
1 (866) 928-1240

Because of the dynamic nature of the Internet, any web addresses or
links contained in this book may have changed since publication and
may no longer be valid. The views expressed in this work are solely those
of the author and do not necessarily reflect the views of the publisher,
and the publisher hereby disclaims any responsibility for them.

Scripture quotations are from The Holy Bible, English Standard
Version® (ESV®), copyright © 2001 by Crossway, a publishing ministry
of Good News Publishers. Used by permission. All rights reserved.

Any people depicted in stock imagery provided by Thinkstock are models,
and such images are being used for illustrative purposes only.
Certain stock imagery © Thinkstock.

ISBN: 978-1-4908-3202-9 (sc)
ISBN: 978-1-4908-3204-3 (hc)
ISBN: 978-1-4908-3203-6 (e)

Library of Congress Control Number: 2014905780

Printed in the United States of America.

WestBow Press rev. date: 3/27/2014

To my son, Steve,
who sharpens my thinking

— Contents —

—— Introduction ——

We are told that in the world today there remain 7,163 unreached people groups. These groups consist of 2.88 billion people or 41 percent of the world's population[1] (Joshua Project 2013). It is staggering to picture this many people living life without the glorious message of the grace and forgivingness of the Lord Jesus. It is overwhelming to think that among these people there is no indigenous community of believers sufficiently large enough or with enough resources to share the gospel with them.

This stunning picture causes us to ask questions such as "How can we reach them?" and "What do we need to do to reach them?" At first glance, these appear to be good questions. They appear to be the right response to the need, especially since we enjoy the gospel and its eternal promises and want others to experience the same. But are these the right questions?

As I was sitting in a Vancouver, B.C. restaurant enjoying supper and fellowship with K. P. Yohannan, I heard him tell me that although these might be useful questions, they are not the right questions. He suggested that the typical answer to these questions puts us in the center of the equation. Instead of focusing on what

---

[1] According to the Joshua Project (www.joshuaproject.net/definitions.php), "An unreached or least-reached people is a people group among which there is no indigenous community of believing Christians with adequate numbers and resources to evangelize this people group."

might be best practices to reach the unreached, our answers tend to revolve around what best practices are for us. Our answers are couched in what fits our agendas or programs or planning.

I have thought about this a lot since then, and found it to be true—too often, brutally true. We like to be in the center of the story. We like to feel good about what we are doing to reach the unreached. We like to tell others about our travels and exploits. We like to feel important and successful in what we have set out to accomplish. We like to do nice things that remove the guilt we often feel about our disproportionate level of comfort and wealth compared with the rest of the world.

There is something else that is brutally true. For many Western believers, missions are a "holy cow." Just like the holy cows of Nepal and India that are to be respected and allowed to wander at will and not be corralled, missions and missionaries are not to be doubted or questioned. If someone tells us they have been called by God into missions, we are to respect that call and never question it. I am sorry to say that even though I grew up in the cowboy city of Calgary, Alberta, I am not very good with cows. A young man came to my office once to inform me that he had been called into missionary work. Rather than admire that call, I asked him how he knew he was called. His response was interesting. He told me he did not like his job, he didn't want to go back to school, and he had been bitten by the travel bug. I think I killed the "holy cow" when I told him he had just given me three reasons why he should not go into missionary work.

When missionaries report what they have or have not been doing, we are not to quiz them about the validity of their activities or the efficacy of their ministries. To question them is to doubt their validity or corral their independence. I am sorry, but I have confronted many such "holy cows" by asking stewardship questions related to strategy, effectiveness, and the use of precious resources such as time and funding.

I think K. P. was right. We do not ask the right questions.

Instead of asking how we can reach the unreached, we ought to be asking, "How can the unreached be reached?" We need to take ourselves out of the center of the equation as well as set aside our "holy cows" so that the unreached will become reached. We need to put the unreached in the center of the equation and seek the best methods and means to see that all unreached people will clearly hear the gospel.

This writing is an attempt to explore the question of how we can get beyond ourselves to effectively participate in reaching the unreached. Each chapter is a call to examine what we have been doing and perhaps point us to what might be done as we seek to get beyond ourselves. To help promote the discussion, a summary of the key principles can be found at the end of each chapter. You will also find a list of questions designed to help individuals and, better yet, church leaders or missions committees apply the principles to their own ministries.

There are two things that have shouted loudly at me as I have written this book. The first is how little I really know about missions and how much more there is to learn. The second is how hard it is for me to get beyond myself. As you read, I trust you will be urged to continue to learn and grow as well.

— Chapter 1 —

By Refocusing on the Purpose of Missions

How do we get beyond ourselves to reach the unreached? To address this question adequately, we need to start at the beginning. Having grown up in a construction family, I understand the value of building a good foundation. That process begins with staking the site, leveling the ground, setting the forms, and pouring the foundation on which the building will rest.

In today's world of missions, it seems to me that the foundation is not clear. If we were to ask various missions groups why they exist and what they are attempting to do, we would hear a myriad of answers, including feeding the hungry, healing the sick, teaching the uneducated, assisting with business development, and providing clean water. These are all admirable goals, but I wonder if in the cacophony of answers we have lost the core purpose, or the bigger picture, of missions.

It reminds me of the fictional story of two bricklayers who were laboring on the construction of a great cathedral. When the first man was asked what he was doing, he responded with something like, "I am laying bricks." When the second was asked what he was doing, his answer was, "I am building a cathedral!"

When I ask mission leaders and missionaries what they are doing, I hear a lot of the first man's response: they describe individual activities rather than the grand purpose. Perhaps that is because we have lost something of the heart of missions. Perhaps we need to go back to the blueprints to see the grand picture and then once again lay a solid foundation on which we can build.

Making Disciples

What does the Bible say about missions? It is among these well-worn words of Jesus to his early disciples that we catch a glimpse of the big picture: "And Jesus came and said to them, 'All authority in heaven and on earth has been given to me. Go therefore and make disciples of all nations, baptizing them in the name of the Father and of the Son and of the Holy Spirit, teaching them to observe all that I have commanded you. And behold, I am with you always, to the end of the age'" (Matthew 28:18–20).

Just before he returned to the Father, Jesus made it clear to the disciples what would come next for them. Here in Matthew, as well as in Mark 16:15, Luke 24:47, and John 20:21, Jesus launches them into the great adventure of missions. This adventure always involved going, and that going would move them beyond themselves into ever-widening circles of contact that would eventually encompass all nations.

The reason for the going was always to make disciples. That was and is today the whole point of missions. That is the cathedral to be built. Although there are many activities that go into disciple-making, including baptizing and teaching, the central purpose is to make disciples.

When we add to the conversation the words of the Holy Spirit through the apostle Paul, we find that central to making disciples is proclaiming gospel. In Romans 10:14 Paul writes, "How then will they call on him in whom they have not believed? And how are they to believe in him of whom they have never heard? And how are they to hear without someone preaching?" We cannot make disciples without proclaiming the gospel, and that proclamation must come in more than the nonverbal communication of good deeds. It must come with clear words that are adorned with good deeds. All our bricklaying must be coupled with clear proclamation.

But what does it mean to make disciples? At the close of the book of Psalms, that wonderful book of prayer and praise, we find Psalm 150:6, which reads, "Let everything that has breath praise the Lord! Praise the Lord!" As David Platt reflects on this in *Finish the Mission,* he writes, "There are an estimated seventeen thousand people groups on the planet, and God deserves praise from every single one of them."[2]

John Piper declares, "Missions is a cross-cultural movement aimed at helping people stop making much of themselves and start making much of their Creator. Missions is a cross-cultural effort to transform people's hearts so that God is felt to be more praise-worthy than sport stars or military might or artistic achievements or anything else that God has made. Missions is a cross-cultural endeavor to help people experience God as their Treasure above all earthly treasures forever. It is a life and death struggle to give people eternal life, which consists in knowing and enjoying God forever."[3]

Making disciples is all about helping people everywhere worship and praise God; it is not about clean water, health care, better farming methods, literacy, or learning to speak English. If we do these things without proclaiming the gospel, we are only raising people's standard of living and making them a little more comfortable on their journey toward eternal condemnation. Our proclamation must be adorned with good works, but good works without proclamation is not missions.

Although we can applaud the conversations that various mission agencies have had about moving toward a more holistic ministry, far too often this has meant a spreading gap between proclaiming the gospel and doing good works without the gospel.

---

[2] Piper and Mathis, 2012, 47.
[3] Piper, 2003.

Why has this happened? Perhaps it is because Paul', words are found to be too realistic. He said, "The word of the cross is folly to those who are perishing" (1 Corinthians 1:18).

Who wants to try to win people's hearts with a foolish-sounding message? Who wants to attempt to break into a community with a message that points out the tragic eternal result of sin? Who wants to communicate a message of man's incompetence and God's grace to an audience living in a culture that pours great effort into worshipping their gods? It is so much nicer to be accepted and applauded by the host culture than to be rejected. Hence we focus on good works with a hope that those works will create opportunities to share the gospel in a nonoffensive way.

The problem with this drift is that Paul, in the same verse, goes on to tell us, "but to us who are being saved it is the power of God" (1 Corinthians 1:18). In Romans 1:16 Paul declares, "For I am not ashamed of the gospel, for it is the power of God for salvation to everyone who believes."

Every person's central and greatest need is the inevitability of suffering God's wrath because of their rebellion against Him. Clearly proclaiming the gospel addresses this need and comes with God's power to change lives.

Too often we are a bit ashamed of the gospel. It feels and sounds far more noble and acceptable to be activists in social causes. Yes, we want to be salt and light in difficult places, but it is much easier to just silently do our good deeds. In doing so, however, we miss the central purpose of missions. We must put the preaching of the cross front and center. Our proclamation of the gospel must also be adorned with good works, but we must not and dare not focus on the latter without the former, lest we continue to fail in the God-given assignment to go and make disciples.

Why do I say "continue to fail"? George Verwer once made this stunning statement: "Statistics show that a quarter of North American cross-cultural missions are currently engaged in translation, evangelization, church planting and teaching. Three-quarters are assigned to administration and support work ... such as agriculture, aviation, community development, literacy, medicine, and relief efforts."[4] Not only that, but more than 87 percent of all cross-cultural missionaries labor among nominally Christian groups. Less than one penny of every dollar of Christian giving to all causes goes toward pioneer church planting among the least-reached people groups.[5]

Addressing social issues, welfare problems, and political tensions is not the church's primary mandate. Although individual Christians ought to concern themselves with being salt and light in the various marketplaces of life and thus address community concerns and issues, the church as a corporate body must not lose sight of its purpose and priority. The social and political climate and the community agenda ought never to cloud or confuse the church's agenda. The church's primary mandate or mission is preaching the gospel to win men and women to Christ and congregate them into churches.

Creating Gathered Communities

This leads us to the second part of our assignment from Jesus. According to Jesus' mandate, making disciples must also include creating gathered communities or churches. It is not enough to evangelize and move on.

Jesus said, "Go therefore and make disciples of all nations, baptizing them in the name of the Father and of the Son and of the Holy Spirit" (Matthew 28:29). Baptism serves as both a public declaration of one's faith and admission into or adoption by a local gathering of believers. Baptism symbolizes our union with Christ in his death, burial, and resurrection (see Romans 6:3–4 and Colossians 2:12).

---

[4] Verwer, 2000, 127.
[5] "Status of World Evangelization," *Joshua Project: www.joshuaproject.net/assts/handouts/status-of-world-evangelization.pdf/* (March 2013).

Grudem writes, "When the candidate for baptism goes down into the water it is a picture of going down into the grave and being buried. Coming up out of the water is then a picture of being raised with Christ to walk in newness of life. Baptism thus very clearly pictures death to one's old way of life and rising to a new kind of life in Christ."[6]

Although one comes into the community of the redeemed by salvation only through faith, baptism is the external act that declares allegiance to Jesus Christ. As such it serves as a public declaration to the rest of the church family that the person being baptized is one of them. It declares the connection with the body of Christ and its particular local gathering.

Becoming a disciple means more than merely being a convert. Paul Borthwick writes, "In the last century, the global church has excelled in making converts and fostering decisions. Evangelistic sermons, literature and films have introduced millions to the gospel story. Many have made an initial response. We have not done a great job in making disciples, however, either in North America or in the Majority world. The person who raises his or her hand at the end of a presentation might be a convert but not a disciple. Jesus didn't say go into the world and make *converts*; he said go into all the world and make *disciples*."[7] Moving from being a convert to being a disciple includes participating in a church community.

Paul's example in the book of Acts demonstrates that everywhere he preached the gospel, he formed a group or community of believers that publicly declared their allegiance to Christ and to fellowship with each other. Today we call that church planting. After Paul left, he sent these churches letters, further explaining the gospel and helping them shape their thinking and behavior to reflect the grace and glory of God.

The importance of church planting cannot be overlooked in

---

[6] Grudem, 1994, 968.
[7] Borthwick, 2012, 50–51.

the purpose of missions. Ott and Wilson emphasize this when they write, "Evangelical missiologists have increasingly emphasized holistic mission and the kingdom of God while rarely even mentioning church planting. While this emphasis may reflect a correction of earlier imbalanced evangelical views, the neglect of church planting in current theologies of mission is also in need of correction. Because the church itself is central to God's mission, church planting must be central to that mission."[8]

Peter echoes the Old Testament to remind us of God's ongoing purpose in creating a community of people: "But you are a chosen race, a royal priesthood, a holy nation, a people for his own possession, that you may proclaim the excellencies of him who called you out of darkness into his marvelous light. Once you were not a people, but now you are God's people; once you had not received mercy, but now you have received mercy" (1 Peter 2:9–10).

"The church becomes the instrument of God's glory and eternal plan, as Paul writes, so that through it the wisdom of God may become manifest, not only to the nations but to rulers and authorities in heavenly places" (Ephesians 3:10).[9] It is through the church and its local gatherings, sometimes huddled together in hidden groups and sometimes gathered in mega-crowds, that God will declare his glory and grace. God has prescribed that his mission moves forward from church to church to church as new communities are formed. In this way, missions are based on churches, not just on individuals.

The local church has been given the authority and responsibility for missions. This is not to be left to individual plan or design. Too often, through the fault of the church as a corporate body, missions and evangelism have been left up to individual concern and motivation. It has become an optional activity that we know we should be involved in but rarely are. Evangelism has become something the "called" do. The church's ingredient has deteriorated

---

[8] Ott and Wilson, 2011, 20.
[9] Ibid., 21.

into supporting missionaries who are forced to travel from church to church begging for what often turns out to be sporadic prayer and meager finances.

The church as a body has been given the mandate to reach the world with the gospel. But prayer and financial support are only the beginning. The local church must also participate in the choosing, training, equipping, strategizing, and sending of missionaries to new neighborhoods and communities, both near and distant.

In describing John Calvin as a churchman, historian Stephen Nichols notes the following about current life in our part of the world:

> In today's Christian environment we can live our entire Christian lives from start to finish without ever passing through a church door. There's Christian radio, Christian television, even entire Christian satellite networks, and many Christian sites on the Web. There are evangelistic crusades and rallies in stadiums. There are Christian bookstores and magazines. Not to mention the ascendancy of parachurch organizations in the current Christian culture. Everything you need for the Christian life can be had without ever entering a church. Such realities would surely grieve Calvin. He simply couldn't conceive of Christianity without the church. He couldn't think of living the Christian life without being rooted in and connected to the local church.[10]

The local church is God's plan for reaching the world. But we incorrectly attempt to export our cultural brand of Christianity and initiate ministry strategies that do not result in the formation of local

[10] Nichols, 2007, 76–77.

communities. Instead, we form organizations and structures that are not effective in transforming a community and cannot be sustained when we are no longer able to supply them with personnel or finances.

Growing Biblical Leaders

Therefore, there is a third part to our assignment from Jesus. His instructions in Matthew 28 include the words of verse 20: "teaching them to observe all that I have commanded you." Our assignment begins with making disciples through proclaiming the gospel and moves toward the formation of local church communities and now extends to teaching these communities to observe or obey all that Jesus commanded.

Paul reinforces this when he writes to Timothy, "You then, my child, be strengthened by the grace that is in Christ Jesus, and what you have heard from me in the presence of many witnesses entrust to faithful men who will be able to teach others also" (2 Timothy 2:1–2). Who were these faithful men Timothy should teach? In 1 Timothy 3:2, Paul describes those qualified to be church elders as men who were "able to teach." Although Timothy was to teach sound doctrine to the entire church family, it seems the specific focus of his teaching was for the shepherds and leaders of the church family. Today, this is called leadership development.

What was Timothy supposed to teach those who were to lead the church family? A brief survey of 1 and 2 Timothy reveals that his teaching topics were to include the following:

1. Sound doctrine (1 Timothy 1:3–4; 4:6–11; 6:2b–10; 2 Timothy 4:1–2)
2. Prayer for all people and those in authority (1 Timothy 2:1–4)
3. The character qualities necessary for those who desired to be leaders (1 Timothy 3:1–13)
4. Warnings about the coming of false teachers (1 Timothy 4:1–4; 2 Timothy 3:1–9; 4:3–5)

5. How to behave in the community of believers (1 Timothy 51–6:2a)

6. Learning to trust God rather than financial wealth (1 Timothy 6:17–19)

7. How to have a long-term perspective while enduring suffering (2 Timothy 2:8–13; 3:10–16)

An examination of the writing order of Paul's letters will reveal a teaching model. In his early letters he sought to introduce a code of conduct for Christian living in a non-Christian environment. Paul sought to establish the new believers and churches in the gospel and its implications. These letters issue a call for believers to please Christ in every area of their personal lives.

In the prison epistles, Paul shows believers how they fit into God's eternal plan. In them, he lays out the significance of the church as God's only plan for the progress of the gospel. He carefully instructs believers in how to conduct their church lives.

His later or pastoral epistles are primarily notes to church leaders, in which Paul gives careful instruction about the church community and the careful selection and training of leaders who will carry on the work into the next generation.

This unfolding revelation of truth is the same in the discipleship process of the believer. One must first understand the gospel and its everyday implications. Next, one must understand the church community and how it fits into God's unfolding plan. Finally, one needs to understand and prepare for participating in or even leading the believing community.

What does this mean? Simply this: The study of Scripture must be central to leadership development. The Word of God was the most important thing Timothy taught potential leaders. Once they understood the enduring principles of God's Word, they would be able to apply it appropriately to their cultural context.

This is important to notice because the leadership development training that is often exported from North America is soaked in our own culture. Instead of teaching leaders how to correctly handle God's Word, we teach them how to do ministry like us. But often our models do not fit their cultural context.

On a visit to the Philippines, I was invited to preach at a small local church. When my friend and I arrived at the church facility, we were warmly welcomed. The music was alive and enthusiastic, and we were refreshed by the exuberance of our brothers and sisters as they heartily praised our wonderful Lord. After about twenty or thirty delightful minutes of worship, the young pastor got up and announced that they were going to begin the worship service. As tattered English-language hymnals were handed out, I turned to my friend and quietly asked what we had just experienced. I thought we were already having a worship service, but apparently not. When I received a copy of the hymnal and opened the front cover, I noticed the sticker announcing that it had once belonged to a church in the midwestern United States. The pastor announced the hymn number, and the pianist began to play the song at a snail's pace. The congregation began to sing, but it seemed painful. The previous joyful enthusiasm had evaporated. What happened? Someone had exported Western church life to this community in the form of a pastoral training program that made the national leaders look and feel like their teachers. Cultural Christianity had been exported at the expense of teaching biblical principles that the students could apply to their culture. I became convinced then and there that we must get beyond ourselves. Our leadership training must focus on Bible teaching, allowing the new leaders to make appropriate application within their cultural context.

We must get beyond ourselves and see the grand picture. We are not in the business of building a program or institution with our name on it. We are not to be busy with ministry activity unconnected to the mandate we have from Jesus. We are to be about the purposeful business of our Lord, who has given us an assignment to go to the world with the message of his grace. Our priorities and activity must conform to his mandate.

Summarizing the Principles

1. The primary purpose of missions' activity is to make disciples.
2. Making disciples must also include the creation of gathered communities or churches.
3. Our assignment extends to teaching these communities to observe or obey all that Jesus commanded.
4. A significant degree of teaching needs to be focused on leaders who in turn can teach others.
5. The teaching of leaders must center on God's Word, allowing them to make appropriate application to their culture.

Questions to Consider

1. What is your church's understanding of the purpose of missions?
2. How do the practices of your church support that purpose?
3. Does your church have a clearly defined list of missions' priorities? If so, what are they? If not, what should they be?
4. Does your church make mission decisions based on emotional appeal, on personalities, or according to clearly understood priorities?

──Chapter 2──

By Asserting the Authority of Scripture

S mall-group Bible studies are fun. The coffee is great. The goodies are a treat. And the stories of the adventures or misadventures of the last week keep us amused. Even the Bible study time can be quite entertaining. Typically the leader tells us to turn to the passage we will be studying. After the rustle of pages or the clicks of the digital media, we find the passage and begin to read it, taking turns around the circle. There may be an opening question designed to catch our attention, but eventually we get down to studying the passage in search of the answer to this question: "What does the passage mean to you?" At this point we scramble to find some way to understand what we think the passage means and explain it to others in our group. The result: We have as many meanings as we have participants, leaving us confused as we say goodbye and head to our homes bewildered about the Bible.

What Does It Mean to Me?

This doesn't just happen in our small-group Bible studies. This is also played out in many parts of the missions world. A number of mission organizations strongly encourage team members to practice a similar form of spiritualizing the text using a method called Lectio Divina. Using a five-step process, this form of Bible reading puts readers at the center and encourages them to find out what a particular Bible verse means to them. Step one is silence, in which readers prepare their hearts to hear from God by slowing down and settling themselves in a quiet place. Step two is reading. Readers choose a passage and read it slowly, even reading it out loud. They read it one or more times with openness to whatever God wants to show them.

Step three calls for meditation where participants read the passage again, this time listening for a word or phrase that stands out to them. They pay attention to the feelings that come as they read the passage. They meditate on the word, phrase, or emotions that came to mind. As they repeat the word or phrase several times, they ponder what God seems to be saying and how it connects with their lives right now. Some proponents of this process tell the participants not to be academic or worry about the context of the passage. Step four is prayer. The reader responds to God by praying their chosen passage, asking God to bring clarity and meaning to the word, phrase, or feeling. They ask God for a deeper understanding of their feelings and what action or attribute they are to embrace. The process closes with step five—contemplation. Here the reader is to rest and wait patiently in God's presence. They are to listen to God as He clarifies what that word, phrase, or emotion means to them for that particular day, committing themselves to respond to God's direction.

This approach is called "spiritualizing" because it seeks to find a deeper, hidden spiritual meaning in the text beyond the obvious meaning. Instead of seeking what the author intended, this method projects the reader's meaning onto the text. The discovered deeper meaning is usually a product of the reader's imagination or the projection of other biblical truth onto the text. In the latter case, the spiritualized meanings can be true statements, but they are true because of other biblical texts and not because of the one being studied.

This approach has also been called the "subjective approach" because it emphasizes what is important for the reader. Scripture's meaning is said to be found in what God says to the reader's heart and mind.

Do you see the problem? Reading and studying the Bible this way puts us in the center. Scripture becomes about us and how we feel and think. We take on the role of defining God's intent. What we think or feel about a Scripture passage becomes authoritative. As a result, the Scripture's inherent authority is undermined and reduced or restricted by our feelings or thoughts, diluting the abiding message of God's Word. As a result, a Scripture passage could mean opposite things to different people.

This kind of thinking is a product of our society. R. C. Sproul comments on the change in attitude toward religion:

> There seems to be a growing outcry about the negative influence of religion in American culture. Religion is held to be the force that keeps people trapped in the dark ages of superstition, their minds closed to any understanding of the realities of the world that science has unveiled. More and more, religion seems to be regarded as the polar opposite of science and reason. It is as if science is something for the mind, for research, and for intelligence, while religion is something for the emotions and for the feelings.[11]

The result of this cultural thinking, Sproul says, "seems to be that in matters of religion, truth is insignificant. We learn truth from science. We get good feelings from religion."[12] In addition, when we add the overlay of relativism that fills our classrooms, truth is no longer absolute. What is truth for one person may not be

---

[11] Sproul, 2012, 6.
[12] Ibid.

truth for another person. We have developed the ability to live with inconsistent "truth" in our communities and even within our own minds. The effect of this on our reading and study of the Scriptures is contentment with relative and even contradictory interpretations built on our opinions and feelings.

The high view of Scripture as the inerrant, authoritative, and sufficient Word of God has begun to evaporate. The Bible no longer stands as the absolute standard that measures all other truth claims. The plain meaning of the words are redefined by the reader.

But this ought not to be! According to Sunder Krishnan, "We live in an age when words have lost their meaning. And so the first thing we have to do if we are going to learn to love the Lord our God with all our hearts, and to love the law as well, is to begin to recapture the original meaning of the language of the Bible. We've got to learn again a new vocabulary—without redefining it, psychologizing it or socializing it." [13]

The Bible Is the Word of God

If we are going to reach the unreached and disciple them with a clear, consistent, timeless message, we need to get beyond ourselves in our handling of Scripture. Although this is not a book on hermeneutics or Bible study methods, we need to reaffirm some basic convictions about our Bible.

The first is this: The Bible is the Word of God in both the Old and New Testaments. "It is inspired by God and therefore unique, different from all other books,"[14] says T. Norton Sterrett. Going on, he says, "To put it simply, what the Bible says, God says. To understand the Bible, you must be confident that it is God's Word, through which he has spoken to human beings, including you.

---

[13] Krishnan, 2003, 22.
[14] Sterrett and Schultz, 2010, 31.

You must affirm that the Bible's statements are authoritative and trustworthy, that you can depend on them without question."[15]

Later, Sterrett writes, "Not everything that people think the Bible says is what God is actually saying in the Bible. Many people have silly or wild ideas. Just because we believe the Bible does not mean that all of our ideas concerning it are necessarily true or that our understanding of a particular verse is correct. This is one of the main reasons why we need to interpret carefully."[16]

The Bible is the inspired, inerrant, authoritative Word of God. It is the rule and governor of all we believe and do, in both our personal and ministry lives. It is the book that measures and judges all we are, do, and say. It stands above every other writing and is the voice of God that we must listen to and obey. As a result, we ought to be very diligent and careful as we study God's Word. Paul told Timothy, "Do your best to present yourself to God as one approved, a worker who has no need to be ashamed, rightly handling the word of truth" (2 Timothy 2:15). Sloppiness in handling Scripture will surely bring judgment on us as we stand ashamed before our Lord.

The second essential conviction is that the Bible is its own interpreter. One passage throws light on another, and a passage must be studied in light of the complete context of a chapter, a book, and the entire Bible. If you have purchased real estate, you have discovered that the basic rule of a good purchase is "location, location, location." The basic rule of good Bible study is just like it: context, context, context. The careful examination of the context of any given passage contains the key to its meaning. Our feelings and ideas do not matter. What matters is the meaning in the original context in which it is found. Most poor interpretations and, worse yet, heretical teachings come from violating this rule of Bible study.

The third conviction is that studying the Bible must be accompanied by obedience. The Bible carefully warns about listening and

---

[15] Ibid.
[16] Ibid.

not obeying (Luke 6:46–49, James 1:22–25). The Bible is not a story or the ramblings of opinionated authors. It is the Word of God that must be understood and obeyed. It is not a message that we can take or leave, depending on how we feel about a particular passage on a particular day. It is the very breath of God that stands as our absolute authority and must be obeyed.

The Aim of Good Interpretation

The aim of good interpretation is quite simple: to get at the plain meaning of the text. What did the passage mean to the original reader? What timeless principles need to be understood and followed by every person in every time frame and in every cultural context? There are a myriad of applications, but there is only one meaning. The task of the interpreter is to discover what the author intended the original readers to understand. There may be more than one application of the principle, but there is only one meaning. What a passage means ought to be the same for everyone who reads and studies it. How it is applied will be as varied as the number of people seeking to apply it.

We do not need to try to find something new or unique. Gordon Fee and Douglas Stuart put it this way:

> The aim of good interpretation in not uniqueness; one is not trying to discover what no one else has seen before. Interpretation that aims at, or thrives on, uniqueness can usually be attributed to pride (an attempt to "out clever" the rest of the world), a false understanding of spirituality (wherein the Bible is full of deep truths waiting to be mined by the spiritually sensitive person with special insight), or vested interests (the need to support a theological bias). Unique interpretations are usually wrong. This is not to say that the correct

> understanding of a text may not often seem unique
> to someone who hears it for the first time. But it is
> to say that uniqueness is not the aim of our task.[17]

The work of the interpreter is to understand and explain the intended thought of the authors of Scripture as disclosed in the actual language used, and understood in the natural and historical context in which it was written. This approach accepts the Bible as it is with the goal of interpretation to understand what it says, not explain it away. It seeks the meaning of Scripture primarily in its open declaration rather than in some mystical, symbolic or sub-surface teachings. It is grammatical and seeks the meaning conveyed in the language as it is understood in its normal grammatical significance. It is historical in that it seeks to understand the language of Scripture within the historical context in which it was written. It advocates the normal use of language, seeking a literal interpretation.

What's This Got to Do with Missions?

Why do we need to talk about this in a book about missions? It is because of an accelerating drift from the inspiration, inerrancy, and authority of the Scriptures in our "evangelical" community. Many people think our opinions and ideas are just as significant as, or even more significant than, the text of Scripture. We have renewed discussions on the validity of the creation story in Genesis 1 and 2. We hear the wonderful truth of substitutionary atonement being questioned and even shunned because it sounds so harsh and unloving. The gospel has become a message about our health, comfort, and prosperity. The message of the Bible is diluted with our feelings. The Scripture's commands become arbitrary. Our personal viewpoint becomes the authority for what is true. The

---

[17] Fee and Stuart, 1981, 14.

biblical authors are seen as expressing opinions we are free to argue with, ignore, or reject.

What kind of a gospel does this leave us? What have we got left to proclaim with authority? How can we plant churches and grow strong biblical leaders without anchoring them to the authoritative Word of God? How do we know that our feelings and the voices we hear when we meditate are from God? If we undermine the authority of Scripture, we merely become another man-made, man-adjusted religion.

We need to get beyond ourselves and our feelings and opinions as we read, study, and proclaim the truths of the Bible. We have a solid foundation to stand on, one that was written by God's hand. Paul says, "All Scripture is God-breathed" (2 Timothy 3:16). It is the very breath of God. It is not made up merely of the words of Moses, the songs of David, the sermons of Isaiah, the recollections of the disciples, or the letters of Paul. It is the very breath of God! These are the very words of God spoken through the words, personalities, and writing styles of those whom He chose to write.

We need to hold to a high view of Scripture, one that compels us to study it carefully and to declare it clearly. This is God's Word, for which we do not need to be ashamed or apologize.

Some time ago, I received a phone call from a very irate woman. I had written a newspaper article that upset her. I knew she was very serious, because her call was long distance at a time when such calls were significantly more expensive than they are now. The lady made it very clear to me, using words I dare not repeat, that I was arrogant and intolerant. I listened to her until she ran out of steam and then told her that I agreed with her. The phone went silent. Then I said, "I don't like what God says either. I also wish it was different. But he is God and I am not, and your argument is not with me but with him. I am just his messenger and it is my task to declare what he has said in his Word." I am not sure I made a friend that day, but the lady calmed down, and we were able to have a pleasant conversation about the wonders of the gospel.

When we lower our view of Scripture, we begin to observe it with suspicion. We ask the same question that Satan asked Eve in the garden: "Did God really say that?" When the pressure to be politically correct squeezes us, it is all too easy to compromise or simply ignore the harder truths of the Bible. Our theological grid becomes our culture, our comfort, and our feelings. We become the final standard for faith and practice. Our decisions about missiology, strategy, and ministry activity become divorced from God's Word. Instead of asking, "What does the Bible say about this?" we ask "What do you think about this?"

I remember participating in a denominational study group tasked with thinking through how to grow the next generation of leaders. The focus of one session was to build a description of a good leader, and group members offered various adjectives that were dutifully recorded on a large flip chart. As I listened, I was reminded of the passages in Timothy and Titus that describe the kind of men to be appointed as elders. When I suggested we look at those texts to help us make our list, I was discouraged by the bemused looks. My comment was completely ignored. But too often that is the way it is. The Bible has lost its place as the foundation of our faith and ministry. We have taken its place.

If we want to reach the unreached, we have to get beyond ourselves and once again assert the Scripture's authority in our lives and ministries. It is the gospel message that will change lives. It is God's Word that is "living and active" (Hebrews 4:12). God has promised that his Word will not return empty or be without influence. He has not made the same promise about our words and our ideas, but only about his Word.

Secondhand Bible

Let's get beyond ourselves and take the time and exert the energy to dig deep into our Bibles. Let's taste and see that the Lord is good. Too many of us are content with someone else's description of what the Word says. We all have our favorite writers, teachers, and preachers. We buy their books, listen to their podcasts, and read their blogs. If they say something, we think it must be true.

In the Introduction to Biblical Studies course I teach, I tell my students that many believers live on the teachings of others rather than have the joy of discovering God and his promises for themselves. I tell them to imagine I have invited them over for dinner. Before their coming, I ask what they like to eat and what they would consider a special treat. Hearing their response, I promise them a fantastic meal. On the day of the dinner appointment, I welcome them into my home and seat them at the table. As they take their places, they see the table decorations and perfect settings, and their expectations are heightened. This is going to be an awesome evening. When it comes time to serve the meal, my wife delivers a plate bearing a delightful arrangement of the promised foods to the table and sets it in front of me. Instead of returning to the kitchen for the other plates, she simply takes her place at the table. Grace is said, and then I begin to taste the various foods on my plate. Not to exclude my guests, I describe to them the texture and taste in great detail. Upon emptying my plate, I get up from the table and invite them to retire to the living room, where we can sit and talk more comfortably.

I know this illustration seems extreme, but this is the experience of the Word for too many believers. They hear another person's description of the delights but never open the Bible and taste it for themselves. Although I wholeheartedly endorse and support preaching and teaching, I equally encourage the development of careful study habits that mine the treasures found in the pages of our Bible.

Most believers I know verbally endorse the need for personal Bible reading and study. But too often it ends with their words. We are far too busy, distracted, or lazy to give ourselves to the study of the Word. We need to get beyond ourselves, because secondhand Bible is not enough. If we want to influence our families, our communities, our nation, and our world, we need to know God's Word. We need to personally dig deep so that the truth we proclaim is not merely what our favorite preacher said, but what we know to be true from our own reading and study.

I had the opportunity to preach in the little church in the village of Scorniceşsti, Romania, the birthplace of communist leader Nicolae Ceauşescu, who lived there until age eleven. As a national leader, he vowed there would never be a church in his village, but there we were, gathered with a handful of believers in a nicely constructed church building. After the service, I discovered that one of the couples was from a neighboring village. There was no church in their village, so each Sunday they left home early in the morning to walk the fifteen kilometers to be with their fellow believers. After the time of worship, teaching, and fellowship, they made the return journey, again on foot. When I asked why they walked so far, they said something I will never forget: "God's Word is worth it."

God's Word is worth it! Let's get beyond ourselves and work hard at handling it correctly so that the millions of unreached will hear clearly hear God's call and not just our opinions and feelings.

Summarizing the Principles

1. The Bible is the inerrant, infallible, authoritative, and sufficient Word of God.
2. The aim of good interpretation is to get to the plain meaning of the text and to surface the principles that need to be understood and followed by every person in every time frame and in every cultural context.
3. When we undermine the authority of Scripture, we alter the gospel message.
4. We need to hold a high view of Scripture, one that compels us to study it carefully and declare it clearly.

Questions to Consider

1. How does your church view the Bible? How important or central is its clear proclamation to your church's purpose and mission?
2. What does your personal Bible study look like? Does your growth in the grace and knowledge of God rely primarily on your study of the Bible or on the writings of others?
3. When did you last inquire about your missionaries' view of the Bible and their practices in studying and declaring its truths? Are they doing their best to present themselves to God as "one approved, a worker who has no need to be ashamed, rightly handling the word of truth" (2 Timothy 2:15)?
4. How can you encourage your missionaries and supply them with resources for their continual study of God's Word?

— Chapter 3 —

By Remembering the Heart of Our Message

At times it is astounding to hear the common misunderstandings of the gospel. If you ask a sampling of Christians to define the gospel you might hear things like this:

- Jesus wants to be your friend.
- God loves you and has a delightful blueprint for your life.
- You need to invite Jesus into your heart and he will bring peace into your life.
- If you just believe, God will take care of all your problems.
- Just accept Christ and he will make you happy and save you from your hassles.

But are these really true descriptions of the gospel? Is this what Jesus' message is all about? It sounds to me like these definitions put us in the very center of the story. They tell us salvation is all about us and our lives. Once again we see how easy and how quickly we make ourselves the focal point of our faith.

Not the Whole Gospel

We all love John 3:16. When I was a kid, we even sang it in Sunday school. "For God so loved the world, the he gave his only Son, that whoever believes in him should not perish but have eternal life." This verse is high on the list of the most well-known verses and is the ultimate "warm and fuzzy" of the Bible. In our witnessing attempts it probably gets quoted more often than any other verse. It is a great verse packed with awesome truth. We are warmed by its emphasis on God's love for the world. We are hugged by the fact that God gave his only Son for us. We are happy to know we just need to believe to have eternal life. This is a wonderful verse! But there is a problem with this verse. All by itself, as it is often quoted, it is not the whole gospel.

In his excellent book *God Has a Wonderful Plan for Your Life,* Ray Comfort spends the first chapter shocking us with the statistical reality that our churches contain many people who do not understand the gospel. Citing research done in 2009 by the Barna Group in the United States he says this:

> Among individuals who describe themselves as Christians, for instance, close to half believe that Satan does not exist, one third contend that Jesus sinned while he was on earth, two-fifths say they do not have responsibility to share the Christian faith with others, and one-quarter dismiss the idea that the Bible is accurate in all of the principles it teaches.
>
> Think for a moment of the implications of such a theology. Here we have millions of "believers" who supposedly confess that Jesus is Lord, and yet think He sinned. They either don't know what the Bible teaches about the Son of God or they believe it is inaccurate when it says that Jesus "knew no sin" (2 Corinthians 5:21), that He was "in all points tempted as we are, yet without sin" (Hebrews 4:15), and that He "committed no sin, nor was deceit found in His mouth" (1 Peter 2:22). Furthermore,

if Jesus sinned, it would mean that he was not the spotless Lamb of God the Scriptures say He was (see 1 Peter 1:19); that His sacrifice was not perfect; and that when God accepted Jesus' death as an atonement for our sins, He sanctioned a "contaminated payment" and is therefore corrupt by nature. Sadly, the multitudes who profess faith in Jesus, yet deny His sinless perfection, appear to be strangers to true regeneration. The Jesus they believe in isn't capable of saving anyone.

In addition, 41 percent of self-proclaimed Christians believe that "the Bible, the Koran and the Book of Mormon are all different expressions of the same spiritual truths—despite the books' vastly contradictory teachings on truth, salvation, and the nature of God. And only 46 percent of born-again adults believe in the existence of moral truth. So that means the other 54 percent don't think that God has moral absolutes, which perhaps explains why so many live their lives as though there is no moral accountability at all.[18]

In a 2012 national study commissioned by the Evangelical Fellowship of Canada Youth and Young Adult Ministry Roundtable, three statements stand out in their summary report on discipleship:

1. Many youth and young adults who are engaged in church activities do not understand the gospel.
2. We may be presenting a superficial understanding of the gospel to youth and young adults.
3. We must repent of transmitting a consumeristic "easy road" understanding of the gospel and seek instead through

---

[18] Comfort, 2010, 10–12.

mentoring and an emphasis on prayer to involve youth and young adults in God's story as it has been told through the ages.[19]

I hope this is not true in the church family you lead or worship with, but if there is even an inkling of this, I think it is time to get beyond ourselves!

The Gospel Is Not About Us

The gospel is not about us! We are not in the center of the story. Nor is God supposed to help us become the hero of the story. In his book, *The Hero*, my son Steve writes:

> Most of us view history as a long collection of short stories. Everyone is writing their own tale, with themselves as the hero. Right now, many obstacles may stand between us and our dreams, but someday we will overcome the challenges, prove the doubters wrong and show ourselves to be the hero that we know ourselves to be. We work to be our own saviour and to overcome our hard circumstances. We try to prove ourselves to be the hero by looking for salvation from our many problems and challenges. Some seek salvation in being wildly successful, others in building wealth and security, others in sexual encounters and still others in gaining power and control. These are just a few ways that people work to overthrow their struggles and be the hero of their own story. We believe that sex, wealth, power and fame will save us from our monotonous life and the trouble

---

[19] Penner et al. 2012, 111.

we face and will show ourselves to be the hero we
know ourselves to be.[20]

What is the result of all this? Lives filled with inadequate saviors
and their broken promises. When the story is all about us, even
"accepting Jesus" and allowing him to be our Savior leaves us as
disappointed as the man who decided to find a solution to his problems by going to church on a particular Sunday morning. He had
made bad financial decisions that led to an inability to pay his rent,
and his landlord had promised to evict him by Tuesday. During the
service he came forward for prayer and prayed to "receive Christ."
In a follow-up phone call on Tuesday morning, he declared he was
no longer a Christian, because Jesus had not provided the money he
needed to pay the rent. The gospel did not meet his needs.

What is the remedy? How do we keep salvation from being
all about us and the comfortable and easy life we would all like to
have? Steve Kroeker answers:

> Instead of seeing ourselves as the hero of our own
> story, we need to flip the script and understand
> our lives in light of God's story. History is not 10
> billion short stories with 10 billion heroes, but is
> one meta-narrative, the one unifying story of God.
> God is the author of history and he invites us into
> his story. He calls us to quit our striving to be the
> hero of our own story, and to define ourselves by
> his story. True meaning, purpose and joy come
> as we find ourselves as minor characters in God's
> grand and sweeping narrative.
>
> In God's story, there is only one Hero. Only
> One can save the day. Only One will overthrow
> evil, rescue the hurting, bring justice and peace

and restore what was lost. Here's a hint: you aren't that hero. You and I aren't the ones who save the day. We are the ones who need rescuing, who need a hero to save us and restore us. In the grand meta-narrative of history, Jesus is the only true Hero. He's the Rescuer that we need.[21]

It seems logical to think we wouldn't have to address this in a book about missions. After all, isn't missionary work about the message of Jesus? Sad to say, for some it is not. For some, the concept of missions is more about doing good things to make people feel better. For some it is about taking care of physical needs and addressing issues of poverty. For some it is about education and upward mobility in the social order. For some it is about freedom from slavery and human trafficking. Although these are all good and even necessary things, they are not the core of missions. Coleman writes, "Christian disciples are sent men and women – sent out in the same work of world evangelism to which the Lord was sent, and for which he gave his life. Evangelism is not an optional accessory to our life. It is the heartbeat of all that we are called to be and do. It is the commission of the Church which gives meaning to all else that is undertaken in the Name of Christ."[22]

As stated earlier, missions are about the proclamation of the gospel adorned with good works. It is not just good works. It is about the cross of Christ. Gilbert issues this caution:

> Indeed I believe one of the greatest dangers the body of Christ faces today is the temptation to rethink and rearticulate the gospel in a way that makes its center something other than the death of Jesus on the cross in place of sinners.

---

[21] Kroeker, 2011, 12.
[22] Coleman, 2009, 125.

The pressure to do that is enormous, and it seems to come from several directions. One of the main sources of pressure is the increasingly common idea that the gospel of forgiveness of sin through Christ's death is somehow not "big" enough—that it doesn't address problems like war, oppression, poverty, and injustice, and really "isn't terribly important," as one writer put it, when it comes to the problems of the world.

Now, I think that charge is altogether false. All those problems are, at their root, the result of human sin, and it is folly to think that with a little more activism, a little more concern, a little more "living the life that Jesus lived," we can solve those problems. No, it is the cross alone that truly deals once and for all with sin, and it is the cross that makes it possible for humans to be included in God's perfect kingdom at all.

Nevertheless, the pressure to find a "bigger," more "relevant" gospel seems to have taken hold of a great many people. Again and again, in book after book, we see descriptions of the gospel that end up relegating the cross to a secondary position. In its place are declarations that the heart of the gospel is that God is remaking the world, or that he has promised a kingdom that will set everything right, or that he is calling us to join him in transforming culture. Whatever the specifics, the result is that over and over again, the death of Jesus in the place of sinners is assumed, marginalized, or even (sometimes deliberately) ignored.[23]

To help our missionaries remember this, we regularly ask them an accountability question: "How many times have you verbally shared the gospel message with others in the last three months?" This is not just for the evangelistic church-planting types. It is also asked of administrators, accountants, teachers, medical personnel, and technical people. This question is for everyone who serves in the missionary endeavor no matter what their official task might be. They have been sent out as ambassadors of Jesus Christ. They

---

[23] Gilbert, 2010, 102–103.

are to be carriers and communicators of the message of the cross. A missionary is one who is sent with a message, not just a skill set or technical training or a passion for people who are hurting. In fact this same question ought to regularly be asked of every believer within the church community.

It can and has been packaged in many different ways, but the heart of the message is simple. It is God to whom we are accountable, and our greatest problem in life is that we have rebelled against God. But he has provided a solution to our sin through the sacrificial death and resurrection of Jesus Christ. We can be included in salvation through repentance and faith.

Don't Forget About Sin

How do we get beyond ourselves? By remembering the heart of the message. Let's go back to John 3:16 for a moment. To understand the gospel, we need to see this verse in its context. "For God so loved the world, that he gave his only Son, that whoever believes in him should not perish but have eternal life." That is the warm and fuzzy part, but here is the part we have forgotten to quote: "For God did not send his Son into the world to condemn the world, but in order that the world might be saved through him. Whoever believes in him is not condemned, but whoever does not believe is condemned already, because he has not believed in the name of the only Son of God" (3:17–18). The gospel is not just about God's love for the world, but about the unspeakable condemnation we face because of our rebellion against God. This is the part of the message that we don't want to talk about, because it makes us feel uncomfortable. We would rather see our family member or neighbor as loved by God than as condemned by God. It is so much easier and makes us feel so much better to think of and speak of love and to do good things in the name of this God who loves us.

All our efforts in missions are not about us, our feelings, or our ideas and programs. They need to be about the fact that apart from the redeeming work of Christ on the cross, all are under the wrath of God for their rebellion against him. The greatest problem of the unreached is not health care, education, poverty, or uncomfortable living conditions. Their greatest problem is the coming judgment of God and his curse on them for their sinful rebellion against him! Jonathan Edwards, in his famous sermon "Sinners in the Hands of an Angry God," got it right. His text was Deuteronomy 32:35, "Vengeance is mine, and recompense, for the time when their foot shall slip; for the day of their calamity is at hand, and their doom comes swiftly." He painted a gruesome picture:

> The God that holds you over the pit of hell, much as one holds a spider, or some loathsome insect over the fire, abhors you, and is dreadfully provoked: his wrath towards you burns like fire; he looks on you as worthy of nothing else, but to be cast into the fire; he is of purer eyes than to bear to have you in his sight; you are ten thousand times more abominable in his eyes, than the most hateful venomous serpent is in ours. You have offended him infinitely more than ever a stubborn rebel did his prince; and yet it is nothing but his hand that holds you from falling into the fire every moment. ...
>
> O sinner! Consider the fearful danger you are in: it is a great furnace of wrath, a wide and bottomless pit, full of the fire of wrath, that you are held over in the hand of that God, whose wrath is provoked and incensed as much against you, as against many of the damned in hell. You hang by a slender thread, with the flames of divine wrath flashing about it, and ready every moment to singe it, and burn it asunder; and you have no interest in any Mediator, and nothing to lay hold of to save yourself, nothing to keep off the flames of wrath,

nothing of your own, nothing that you ever have done, nothing that you can do, to induce God to spare you one moment.[24]

This horrendous need and the amazing message that announces God's grace in sending his Son to take our place in the judgment we deserve is our motivation to go into all the world. The world has no greater need, and we have no greater message. Let's get beyond ourselves and see the true condition of the lost and their need to hear the good news of grace. Let's get beyond our embarrassment. Let's get beyond our tangential programs and ministry agendas and get in line with God's! Let's put the cross back into the center of our mission endeavors. Let's put the message back into the heart of missions.

Our Agenda or God's?

This challenge is not just for long-term missionaries. This ought to also be central to our ministry projects, partnerships, and short-term ministries. In all these decisions we need to ask, "Whose agenda are we following? Our own or God's? Are we involved because it seems like a nice thing to do, or are we involved because it will advance or enhance the gospel? Will our efforts and expense make a difference just for now or for eternity? Will our investment help people come to know the eternal consequences of their sin and the gracious remedy? Or will it only address a relatively temporary problem?" We all know the right answer to these questions, but we need to be brutally honest with ourselves.

One of the noticeable trends among mission organizations is the movement toward hiring successful businessmen to fill the role of executive director. Although there is nothing wrong with successful businessmen, it is wrong when business administration

---

[24] Edwards, 1741.

and efficiencies becoming the primary governing force and motivation for mission activities. My fear is that brokenness over the lost and passion for gospel proclamation gets replaced at the top of the organization with discussions about governance models and best financial practices. When that takes place, marketability and resource management begin to determine ministry activity. Let's face it: some programs are more appealing to donors than others. Contributing to some projects makes us feel better about ourselves. We are results oriented, and alleviating poverty seems a lot more immediate than the long process of presenting the gospel and planting a church. This is not true for just missions; we also do this as we measure success in our own immediate ministries.

Recently a church planter told me that a church plant could be considered successful when 300 people were attending. What does that say about all those churches of 100 or fewer people that are dotted across our country? We need to move beyond ourselves and what seems best in our system of measurement. We need to put the needs of those living under the wrath of God at the center of our activity. "The cross must be central to every dimension of the mission of God's people—from personal evangelism among individual friends to ecological care for creation, and everything in between."[25]

The message of the cross is the greatest message in the world! There seems to be an endless amount of bad news in the world today, plus wars, famines, illiteracy, homelessness, poverty, oppression, slavery, and, and, and … the list could go on and on and on. But we have good news! Not just good news, fantastic news! The best news! In the familiar Christmas story of Luke 2, the angels tell the shepherds, "I bring you good news of great joy that will be for all the people. For unto you is born this day in the city of David a Savior, who is Christ the Lord."

Just think of it. Our sins are no longer counted against us; we

---

[25] Wright, 2010, 43.

have been completely forgiven and no longer face God's condemnation for our rebellion against him. We have been adopted into his forever family and will enjoy the unimaginable glories of his kingdom forever. We not only have good news, but have the assurance of being a part of "a kingdom that cannot be shaken" (Hebrews 12:28). Jesus said, "I will build my church, and the gates of hell shall not prevail against it" (Matthew 16:18). No matter what happens in the world or around us, God will not abandon his promises or fail at building his church. We will face hardship and pain and suffering as we follow Jesus, but it will be through these things that he prepares us for the extravagance of his coming kingdom.

In addition to the joy of our salvation, we have the joy of participating with God in building his kingdom through proclaiming the gospel. God has chosen us to be his messengers, his ambassadors, his representatives through whom the message of his grace will be heard and seen. "But you are a chosen race, a royal priesthood, a holy nation, a people for his own possession, that you may proclaim the excellencies of him who called out of darkness into his marvelous light" (1 Peter 2:9). Through our proclamation we may even have the delight, perhaps in our own generation, of seeing the completion of the task that will bring about Christ's return as declared by his words in Matthew 24:14, "And this gospel of the kingdom will be proclaimed throughout the whole world as a testimony to all nations, and then the end will come."

And when that end comes, God's promise to us will be fulfilled:

> We shall not all sleep, but we shall all be changed, in a moment, in the twinkling of an eye, at the last trumpet. For the trumpet will sound, and the dead will be raised imperishable, and we shall be changed. For this perishable body must put on the imperishable, and this mortal body must put on immortality. When the perishable puts on the imperishable, and the mortal puts on immortality,

then shall come to pass the saying that is written: "Death is swallowed up in victory." "O death, where is your victory? O death, where is your sting?" The sting of death is sin, and the power of sin is the law. But thanks be to God, who gives us the victory through our Lord Jesus Christ. (1 Corinthians 15:51–57)

What can we say to all of this? Paul expresses our only appropriate response this way: "Therefore, my beloved brothers, be steadfast, immovable, always abounding in the work of the Lord, knowing that in the Lord your labor is not in vain" (1 Corinthians 15:51–58). What is that work or labor? Paul tells us in his words to Timothy, "I charge you in the presence of God and of Christ Jesus, who is to judge the living and the dead, and by his appearing and his kingdom: preach the word; be ready in season and out of season; reprove, rebuke, and exhort, with complete patience and teaching" (2 Timothy 4:1–2).

Let's get beyond ourselves and remember and delight in the heart of our message: "Jesus Christ came into the world to save sinners, of whom I am the foremost" (1 Timothy 1:15).

Summarizing the Principles

1. Many "Christian" people in our churches today do not clearly understand the gospel.
2. We need to remember that the heart of our message must address the greatest problem of mankind: our sin and rebellion against God.
3. Regardless of their job description, missionaries need to be held accountable for regularly sharing the gospel message.
4. Resource investment decisions in connection with mission programs, projects, and trips need to be made on how they will enhance and accelerate the proclamation of the gospel.

Questions to Consider

1. What is the gospel? Can you clearly articulate the message of the cross? If you are struggling with this, read Gilbert's *What Is the Gospel?*
2. Can each of your church's missionaries or the missionaries you support articulate the gospel? Have you ever asked them? Perhaps you will want to send each one of them a copy of Gilbert's book.
3. How does your church keep your missionaries accountable to the primary task of preaching the gospel? How do you keep the missionaries you support accountable?
4. On what basis does your church make commitments to mission projects, partnerships, or short-term opportunities? Are those decisions made in terms of how they affect the presentation of the gospel or what fits with current trends?

— Chapter 4 —

By Celebrating and Responding to Globalization

God does amazing things! We really shouldn't be surprised by that, because He is always doing amazing things. He does them because He is amazing. He does them to radiate his glory and display his sovereignty. He does them so that all the nations of the earth will rejoice.

The particular amazing thing I am thinking about is his work in stirring people of the earth to move to new countries and cities. They move because of war, economic struggles, educational needs, job opportunities, and family connections. Although they think they are moving to find a better life, our amazing God is moving them toward the influence of the gospel.

The problem for many of us is that these people from other parts of the world are moving into *our* communities. They are attending our universities. They are shopping in our malls. They are riding on our trains and buses. They are driving on our streets. They are eating in our restaurants. They are working in our marketplaces. They are becoming our medical practitioners and legal experts. They are serving our fast food. They are selling us electronics. They are building our houses. They are teaching our children. They are everywhere. And they look different and smell different and sometimes dress differently. They talk different and view time and work and religion differently. The list of dissimilarities could go on and on.

I remember walking down the hall of my son's high school. On the walls hung pictures of graduating classes dating back to the first class of 1960. As I walked from picture to picture, the names and faces changed from being totally those of white European descent to being a colorful rainbow of Asians. In fact, at his graduation, my son was one of only a handful of non-Asian students. Over the years the neighborhood had changed from a predominantly European—particularly German—community, to one that was increasingly Asian. This is not unique to our neighborhood, but has been repeated over and over again in many communities.

An Annoyance or an Assignment?

Instead of seeing these new faces as an assignment from God, we often see them as an annoyance. Just think about driving for a moment. In our independent, Western law-based society, we have been taught to drive defensively. We know there are rules that must be followed and that we need to look out for ourselves. We must guard ourselves against the inadvertent actions of other drivers. This is not so in many regions of the world. There are many very large cities in the Southern Hemisphere where it seems that government has wasted a lot of money painting lines on the road. They really mean nothing. If the road markings indicate two lanes in a certain direction, you will be certain to find three or even four cars navigating their way side by side with numerous motorbikes also weaving their way among the cars.

And what about all the horn honking? To the North American mind, it is a rude nightmare. But is it? In the community-based cultures of the Southern Hemisphere, driving is not an individualistic event. It is a community event. They are all moving toward their destinations together, and the car horn is the way to let the others know they are there. It is not rude, but a gentle announcement of their presence. In our individualistic culture we are thinking about our personal destination and the time deadline we are under, and the horn means "Get out of my way!" In the community-based culture, it means "I am here; let's watch out for each other." In our individual-istic culture we are very conscious of protecting our vehicle against damage. In the community-based culture, the driver looks out for the front of his vehicle and the other drivers look out for the rear. You do not worry about what is toward the back of your car, just what is ahead. The rest of the community will take care of the back. The problem comes when the two cultural mind-sets merge into the same traffic thoroughfare. The result is we can become quite racist when someone from another culture does not respond like we do.

As we see the hand of God moving people across borders and into our neighborhoods, how do we get beyond ourselves? How do we move beyond our feelings of infringement and insecurity? How do we keep from clinging to our cultural ideals and demanding that everyone else live by them? How do we keep from becoming even silent racists?

Globalization and the Local Church

Let's take it beyond the personal. How does or should globalization affect our church? "So how should the church respond to the move-ment of immigrants today? Do churches see these changes as new avenues of ministry or as problems? Consider what a difference it would make if every immigrant or refugee family was befriended by a local church. What if the first contact every immigrant had in a new city was with a loving group of Christ followers who welcomed them, took them around the city, taught them how to use public transportation, and showed them where the thrift stores were and where the ESL (English as a second language) classes were meeting. Do you think that would make a difference?"[26]

"With these mass migrations of peoples, we have the oppor-tunity to reach people who were, up to this point, considered

---

[26] Swanson and Williams, 2010, 39.

unreached—not because we went to *their* place but because they came to *our* place. The world is changing before our eyes. In Toronto, one of the most international cities in North America, a pastor observed, 'God called us to go to all nations. We didn't go, so he's bringing all nations to us!'"[27]

To get beyond ourselves, we need to celebrate globalization because it is the work of our God! The Scriptures make it very clear that he is sovereign. Through Isaiah God declares, "I am God, and there is none like me, declaring the end from the beginning and from ancient times things not yet done, saying 'My counsel shall stand, and I will accomplish all my purpose'" (Isaiah 46:9–10). In Acts 17:26 Paul tells us that in his sovereignty, God "made from one man every nation of mankind to live on all the face of the earth, having determined allotted periods and the boundaries of their dwelling place."

Everyday people are making decisions about leaving their homeland to find a better life in a new country. Through those decisions God is moving people toward us, and we have unprecedented opportunities to share and live the gospel before them without ever getting on an airplane. "Missions is no longer across the ocean and geographically distant; it is across the street and is culturally distant, in our cities and in cities on all six continents. In reality we have moved from a world of about 200 nations to a new world of some 400 world-class cities."[28] In Acts 17:27 Paul tells us why God has determined the exact places people should live: "that they should seek God, and perhaps feel their way toward him and find him." This migration of people should not be seen as an annoyance, but as an opportunity.

Now, before you simply say, "That's nice," you need to think about God's sovereignty in your life. Why do you live in the community you do? Why do you live on your street? Why do you work

[27] Borthwick, 2012, 40.

[28] Bakke and Sharpe, 2006, 83.

where you work? Why do you have the education you have? Why do you shop where you shop?

It is very easy to give the pragmatic reasons related to our opportunities, decisions, and good fortune. But are those the real reasons? I don't think so. If God is indeed sovereign, which he is, every one of these decisions is under his sovereignty. As believers, we can see every one of these decisions as a specific assignment from God. Paul says, "So, whether you eat or drink, or whatever you do, do all for the glory of God" (1 Corinthians 10:31). To the Colossian church he writes, "And whatever you do, in word or deed, do everything in the name of the Lord Jesus, giving thanks to God the Father through him" (Colossians 3:17). In other words, whatever you do and say at home, in your neighborhood, at your school, or at your place of employment is to be a reflection of the glory of God. It ought to tell the story of God's greatness, glory, and grace. As Osborne reminds us:

> If you are a Christian, you're in full-time ministry. You are a believer-priest on special assignment representing God in everything you do. The only difference between those of us who serve God in full-time ministry and those of us who serve him in the secular marketplace is the organization that pays our salary and the setting in which we carry out our ministry. If you stock shelves at Walmart, run a pool-cleaning service, or crunch numbers in a cubical [sic], you're in full-time ministry. Your assignment is to infiltrate a segment of society that would otherwise go untouched. What you do is every bit as important to the kingdom as anything done by people who get their paycheck from a church or ministry organization.[29]

[29] Osborne, 2012, 177.

So let's move beyond ourselves and our comfort zones and give ourselves to the assignment our Lord has given us.

In light of globalization, what should our churches look like? How can we move beyond ourselves and the programming that is focused on our spiritual comfort? Churches often struggle with the temptation to keep up with the past. Each one has stories of the glory days of their ministry. Each tells of times under different leadership or conditions when they experienced the blessing and excitement of growth. But times have changed; things are not the way they used to be. Part of this is because in many cities, the community has changed. It is no longer filled with people just like us.

In one area of Vancouver the last sixty years has seen the community demographic change from predominantly German to Asian. The German congregations in the community flourished in the 1950s and 1960s but have since faced the demise of the glory days. Such a church can take one of several routes. It can choose the struggle of trying to preserve its cultural identity and in so doing watch the influence of its ministry shrivel. Or it can relocate to a neighborhood, usually suburban, to which their kind has migrated and as a result abandon a community in need of the gospel. Or it can choose to remain in the neighborhood and face the challenge of reorienting its ministry to the new community it finds around itself. The underlying question is this: Will we only coexist with the nations around us or will we see the changing landscape as an opportunity to make an eternal difference in the lives of those God has brought to us?

Bibbey addresses Canadian multiculturalism and the problems that have resulted from official policies of the Canadian government:

> When a country like Canada enshrines pluralism through policies such as multiculturalism and bilingualism and the guaranteeing of individual rights, the outcome is coexistence—no more, no less. But there's a danger. If there is no subsequent vision, no national goals, no explicit sense of

coexisting for some purpose, pluralism becomes an uninspiring end in itself. Rather than coexistence being the foundation that enables a diverse nation to collectively pursue the best kind of existence possible, coexistence degenerates into a national preoccupation. Pluralism ceases to have a cause. The result: mosaic madness.[30]

But the church should be about much more than mere coexistence. If the gospel can break down the colossal cultural and religious barriers between Jew and Gentile (see Acts 15 and Ephesians 2), it can make a significant difference in our globalized communities.

Where Do We Begin?

So, where do we begin? Let me suggest first that we begin by developing a clear sense of purpose for our church's ministry. This is more than just a purpose statement that is hidden away on an official document somewhere. This is a sense of purpose that permeates the church and every one of its ministries. It ought to be one of the guards and guides in decision making and direction setting. It ought to be a measuring tool we use to evaluate the purpose and effectiveness of every one of our ministries. It ought to move us to be more intentional in everything we undertake as a church family.

Second, get to know who lives next door to you. Why do they live next door? Are they here because they are running from bad government? Are they here in pursuit of business opportunities? Have they been drawn from the comfort of their homeland for the sake of their children's education? What do they know about you? What do they know about your faith in Christ? What do they know about your church? Is your church seen as another religion they do

---

[30] Bibby, 1990, 103–104.

not understand? Are they confused by what they see in a country that claims to be "Christian" and yet appears to be so immoral? What do they need? What is it you can do to help them? How can you introduce them to the love of the Lord Jesus Christ and his sacrifice for their sin? What is the best platform you have to declare your interest in them?

It is so easy to sit in our church and enjoy the worship, the teaching, and the fellowship, but never look at the people the Lord has brought into our neighborhoods. It is so much easier to send our missionary dollars overseas but neglect the mission project right next door. Our urban neighborhoods are changing, and we can become commuter churches to which we travel while enjoying the insulation of our car, or we can look creatively at our community and design ministry that will let its people know we are interested in them.

Third, find places outside church meetings to serve the people of the city. We tend to invite people into our church meetings and activities. We plan programs for ourselves and hope to invite others. But we need to go out to the city and serve in practical ways on the street level. It might be cleaning a park or a street, taking food to the poor, volunteering in schools, helping with community events and festivals, or meeting the practical needs of new immigrants. We need to become more visible in the community and not just by building bigger buildings or putting up digital signs with cutesy Christian sayings on them. We need to become visible as people who help and love others. In North America, too often the church is seen only as a group of people who meet in closed buildings but are invisible in the community.

In September 2011 I spent some time in the area of Japan that was affected by the earthquake and massive tsunami that had happened in March. I heard from the victims that while other Japanese people didn't seem to care, the church was very active in helping people rebuild homes and reclaim their lives. Through the tsunami, the church became very visible, and people who previously had little access to the gospel now had believers enter their lives at their greatest point of need and introduce them to Jesus.

Fourth, be prepared to supply resources for the God-given passions of people who enter your ministry. If you want to reach out cross-culturally, ask the Lord to send you someone who has a heart and the capacity to influence a new segment of your community. God's greatest resources are people, and the most effective ministries are launched by people who have a God-given passion. Pray for them. Listen to their hearts. Help shape their ministry passion according to the church's overall purpose and core values and provide the resources and encouragement they need to launch. Every one of the international language ministries in the church I serve was started by a person who came to the leadership team with a passion to reach their countrymen. Our task was to guide them, provide resources for them, and launch them in the pursuit of their passion.

Fifth, to accomplish this well, you need to develop a clear philosophy and strategy for ministry integration. How are you going to reach out? How are the new people going to fit into the life and ministry of your church? How can you create opportunities that will provide new people with a sense of acceptance and participation?

It is very important to avoid building ministry ghettos where people are told to go to their appropriate corners. When we first began to do live translation of our worship services, we did it by hardwiring audio jacks into various sections of the sanctuary. That meant the Chinese had to sit in one place and the Russians in another. But when FM broadcasting became available and we removed the hardwiring, people had the freedom to sit anywhere they wanted.

Just as we need to be very conscious not to push the single or the divorced into a corner by themselves where they have only each other to lean on, so it is with our cross-cultural brothers and sisters. We need to provide significant ministry to them, but we don't want to do that at the expense of their being a part of the larger church family. They must know they are an equal part of the family. Although we want to meet their unique needs and disciple them in the language of their heart, we want to include them in the planning of larger events and in the various arenas of ministry. There are no second-class members in the church. Sometimes we have inadvertently made them feel that way by making decisions that forget or exclude them. But there is no "we" and "they." There is only "us." People may look, smell, and sound different, but once in Christ Jesus, we all are the church and an equally important part of it. We want each person to feel loved and accepted. This demands careful, intentional, and repeated communication.

But let me warn you, multicultural ministry is a messy business. There will be misunderstandings, miscommunication, and misconceptions. People will not fit into the same box. No single program or program format will be effective with each cultural group. One size will not fit all. Flexibility must be the rule. The discussion of spiritual gifts in 1 Corinthians 12–14 teaches us that diversity is not in opposition to unity. There are different gifts but there is one body. There is diversity but one community. Unity must allow diversity, and uniformity will not bring unity. It may look like it outwardly, but there will always be some chafing, which will surface as discouragement, disillusionment, and distrust of the decision makers and the decision-making process. A multicultural ministry will be a dynamic ministry filled with fluidity and change. But it will be exciting as people from across the nations are introduced to the grace of the Lord Jesus and come to love and worship him.

There is another exciting dimension to building a cross-cultural ministry at home. It becomes a great platform for overseas mission projects. We can use the wealth of resources found in cultural understanding and language to remove the barriers to effective service in overseas projects. Since people are the church's greatest resource, a multicultural church has a deep reservoir of cultural expertise, experience, giftedness, and skill available to invest in reaching the unreached. Many will be excited to invest and/or serve in their home countries for the cause of the gospel. Some of them have been sent to us so we can participate in their training and then give them resources as they return to have an effect on their homeland.

Four Kinds of Churches

At the expense of generalizing, it seems to me that when it comes to cross-cultural ministry, there are four kinds of churches. The first is the Community Partnership Church. This church is generally made up of one cultural group. It is an ethnic church whose vision and strategy is largely defined by that culture. It may be a Chinese church, a Korean church, or an English speaking church. It primarily shares the same geographical region with every other church in the community.

The second type of church is the Building Partnership Church. This church has opened its building to another culture. The partnership is defined by a rental contract, and the church usually advertises different worship services at different times in different languages. What the language groups share in common is a building where the dominant culture is the landlord; the ethnic church's value is governed by the benefit or disruption it brings to the landlord.

Church three is the Ministry Partnership Church. This church has become intentionally cross-cultural and works at integration within mutual ministries. The various cultures form one church and are not seen as separate churches or congregations. This model demands a great deal of flexibility and creativity but begins to more closely reflect a small slice of the picture of Revelation 7:9–10 where we are told of "a great multitude that no could number, from every nation, from all tribes and peoples and languages, standing before the throne and before the Lamb, clothed in white robes with palm branches in their hands, and crying out with a loud voice, 'Salvation belongs to our God who sits on the throne, and to the Lamb!'"

The fourth church takes this picture one step further and becomes a Leadership Partnership Church. This church enjoys a multicultural leadership team where culture and language are not dividing lines. Elders are not chosen because they are from a certain part of the world, but because they meet the biblical qualifications outlined by Paul in his letter to Titus and Timothy. Beginning with this model of leadership, the church family does not divide over ethnic differences, but seeks to intentionally reach beyond itself to the wider community and world without cultural bias.

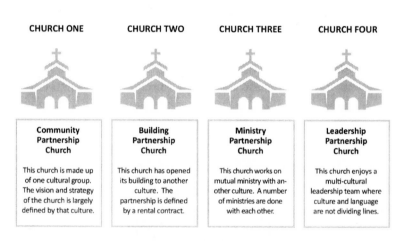

CHURCH ONE	CHURCH TWO	CHURCH THREE	CHURCH FOUR
Community Partnership Church	**Building Partnership Church**	**Ministry Partnership Church**	**Leadership Partnership Church**
This church is made up of one cultural group. The vision and strategy of the church is largely defined by that culture.	This church has opened its building to another culture. The partnership is defined by a rental contract.	This church works on mutual ministry with another culture. A number of ministries are done with each other.	This church enjoys a multi-cultural leadership team where culture and language are not dividing lines.

Although each of these four types of churches has its place, our challenge is not to stay locked in our own cultural comfort zone. The status quo is not acceptable. Unreached pockets of our community will not reach themselves. They need the local church to get beyond itself and intentionally take steps to communicate the gospel to them.

To build a ministry that reaches out to multiple cultures and groups, we need to intentionally deemphasize what divides us and emphasize what ties us together. The differences are real, but whenever we focus on how we are different, we construct sometimes insurmountable walls and barriers. But when we focus on what binds us together, the differences do not become the main point of concern. We need to emphasize that it is the gospel that binds us together. We have a common Redeemer, Bible, and eternal destination. We need to celebrate our unity in Christ Jesus. We serve the same Master and seek to reach out to the same world. We work toward a common purpose, understand a common philosophy of ministry, share common ministries, and are led by a common leadership team. When we see ministry this way, it is no longer about us and we are able to move beyond ourselves.

We need to see something else: the church is not someone else. It is us. It is you. So often pastors and church leaders hear comments that start with, "If the church would do this ..." or "If the church would take care of that ..." and conclude with a description of what the speaker sees as a problem or an issue. When most people say that, they suggest someone else do something about the problem they see or feel. My inward and sometimes outward response to those kinds of comments goes something like this: "Because you are the one who sees or feels the problem, might it be that God is directing you to do something about it? Perhaps the Holy Spirit has caused you to notice the issue or has laid it on your heart because he wants you to lead or participate in finding the solution." Occasionally, when my response is verbal, the conversation ends rather abruptly. But often it inspires a new direction in the mind and heart of the one carrying the concern. So let me remind you that you are the church and caution you with the news that God wants you to be involved in broadcasting the glory of his name. This is not the task of someone else. That task begins with you, and it begins when you get beyond yourselves in your own neighborhood and take seriously the assignments God has given you.

Don't Forget the International Student

Whether we realize it or not, many of the future leaders and influencers of the world are in our communities. "Those international students living, shopping, and studying in our midst are some of the brightest, best connected, and most ambitious from their countries. The 'cream of the crop' comes to the U.S. to study. International students represent the top five percent of the people of their country. Forty-five percent of the current heads of state studied in the U.S."[31] An overwhelming number of graduates from our North American universities become governors, cabinet members, and top influencers in their home countries.

The effect of reaching international students can be far-reaching. When they come to us, internationals pay their way, acquire visas, and speak our language. When internationals return home, they already know their culture and their language, have relationships, hold positions of influence, and are more likely to be effective in countries hostile to Christianity. It's also important to note that the majority of these students come from the upper levels of society. That means they are among those whom traditional missionaries would rarely meet or influence in a personal way.

"Many churches attempt to reach international students through specific ministries or programs. But we could we be even more strategic in how we reach international students in our hometowns? Many of the internationals affected by such ministries were Christians before arriving or had some predisposition to Christianity. These are important people for us to welcome and embrace, to be certain, but there are so many who remain untouched by these ministries, and, more importantly, unexposed to the truth about Jesus."[32]

How can we reach them? Many suggest that one of the best methods is by getting beyond ourselves and opening our homes to them. But sadly, as Tyler Ellis quotes Tom Philips' book *The World at Your Door*, "Statistics prove that among the international students who study in the U.S., historically 70% have never been invited to an American home during their stay. More than 85% are never invited

---

[31] Salem, 2009.
[32] Ibid.

to an American church or have any meaningful contact with genuine Christians during an average stay of four years."[33] Certainly the statistics are comparable in Canada. But this ought not to be—especially since many accompany their luggage with the expectation that by coming to what they think is a Christian country, they will be invited to a church, be given a Bible, and learn something about Jesus.

Let's get beyond ourselves and celebrate globalization by actively reaching out to the world at our door.

---

[33] Ellis, 2013.

Summarizing the Principles

1. Our sovereign God is moving people to places where they can more readily hear the gospel.
2. We live in proximity to new immigrants because God has given us the assignment to reach them with the gospel.
3. We need to rethink the ministry shape of our church to include cross-cultural outreach in its core.
4. One of the greatest places to prepare for long-term overseas ministry is in local cross-cultural ministries.
5. The international students who enter our universities and colleges provide an open door to many parts of the world.

Questions to Consider

1. Who is living in your neighborhood? How does this compare with who is attending your church? Is there a segment of your community that is currently outside the reach of the gospel?
2. What are you doing outside the walls of the church that gives you the opportunity to proclaim the gospel adorned with good works?
3. What is the ministry shape of your church? Is it the kind of place where new people feel welcomed? Or do you put them on the spot or single them out in some way?
4. How can you as an individual, a committee member, or a key leader encourage your church to look beyond itself toward the unreached in your neighborhood?
5. What are you actively doing as a church to reach the international students studying in your community's schools?

— Chapter 5 —

By Commissioning the Right Long-Term Missionaries

I read the story of a university student who declared her passion for reaching China. She prayed regularly for China. She wanted to learn Chinese. She was ready to quit university and go to China immediately. One day she was asked if there were any Chinese students on her campus. She look a bit confused and then answered, "Well, yeah, but they kind of cluster together and they all live in one set of dorms." She was then asked, "Well, have you ever been to the Chinese dorms?" "No," she replied. "They're all the way on the other side of the campus. And they all just stay to themselves!"[34]

I am not sure how this well-meaning young lady missed it, but it sounds all too familiar. Unfortunately this conversation is not unique to her. There are many who feel "called" to a particular people or place, but have not exhibited very many reasons for the church to get excited about participating with them. How can someone think they are going to get on an airplane and fly halfway around the world to reach out to people if they won't even get beyond themselves and cross the city or the campus or the street to reach them? Are people somehow converted partway

---

[34] Hickman, Hawthorne, and Ahrend, 2009, 725.

across the ocean while on their way to a missionary destination? Do people suddenly become evangelists of excellence because they breathe pressurized air at 36,000 feet? Do they miraculously become experts in biblical studies, able to clearly articulate the truths of Scripture because they ate one of those first-rate airline meals? I think not!

Learning from Antioch

To get beyond ourselves, we cannot send anybody out. We cannot even send someone out to the far corners of the planet just because they say they are called. We need to commission the right long-term missionaries. And who are they? I think we can take some cues from the early church in Antioch, whose overseas missionary adventures began in Acts 13. Notice what the text says:

> "Now there were in the church at Antioch prophets and teachers, Barnabas, Simeon who was called Niger, Lucius of Cyrene, Manaen, a lifelong friend of Herod the tetrarch, and Saul. While they were worshipping the Lord and fasting, the Holy Spirit said, "Set apart for me Barnabas and Saul for the work to which I have called them." Then after fasting and praying they laid their hands on them and sent them off. So, being sent out by the Holy Spirit, they went down to Seleucia, and from there they sailed to Cyprus. When they arrived at Salamis, they proclaimed the word of God in the synagogues of the Jews. And they had John to assist them." (Acts 13:1–5)

It is physically impossible for us to visit the ancient city or the church of Antioch, but let's take some time to visit it as we see it in this passage. The first thing we might notice in our tour of the church is its cultural diversity. It would have been a lot of fun to be a part of this colorful cross-cultural church. It was made up of people from various ethnic groups. Barnabas was a Levite from Cyprus. Simeon, called Niger, was a black African. Lucius of Cyrene was from North Africa. Manean was raised with Herod the tetrarch, and Saul was from Tarsus in Cilicia. The leadership group was a snapshot of the vibrant city of Antioch, which was known as the Queen of the East because of its significant location on a major trade route and its resulting prosperity and mixed population. This picture seems to suggest that the church was very active in reaching beyond themselves to the culturally diverse residents.

The second thing we might notice is that the leadership team was made up of "prophets and teachers." Without going into all the details about these two offices, we do know that having them mentioned likely means that proclamation and teaching God's Word was central to this team and to the church.

When we continue our examination, we see that the specific missionary call was not isolated to an individual. It was not just personal to Barnabas and Saul, who then announced it to the church family. Since both the church and its leaders are mentioned in the first verse, it seems most probable that the Spirit led through the entire church. As well, when the two returned home from their first trip, Acts 14:26–27 says they reported to the whole church. This is significant because ministry is not a solo event but an extension of the church family. The later teaching by Paul on the gifts of the Spirit in 1 Corinthians 12 instructs that each gift is recognized as valuable and is needed by the church family. Thus each gift or gifted person does not operate in a void or vacuum but in the context of the entire church family. In other words, for a person to simply announce a call to the ministry is not enough. Such a call needs to be recognized and affirmed by the rest of the church family as they watch the individual serve the church family.

This might seem contrary for those who are familiar and comfortable with the more traditional approach to missions.

The modern missionary movement was launched during a time when the organized church was essentially opposed to reaching those who had never heard. William Carey, known by many as the father of modern missions, founded the Baptist Missionary Society in 1792, with a particular focus on India. The church leaders of Carey's time responded to his missionary passion with, "If God wants to win the heathen, He will do it without us." As the missionary movement grew, those first missionaries were rugged people who heard God's call as individuals and went out with very little support or guidance from their local church. It is out of this pioneering spirit that our understanding of the individualism of the missionary call has grown. Even when local churches later became passionate about supporting missions, the selection of who would go and where they were to go was considered holy business between an individual and God alone. The church's task was not to question the call, but to provide financial support and prayer. The rest of the details were left to the individual and their mission organization.

We certainly respect those who endured great sacrifice and hardship when the church had so little vision—in fact we ought to commend them—but this does not mean the pattern is biblical. The calling and sending of missionaries was never intended to be an individual experience, but is to include the local church family.

As you looked at the account in Acts 13, did you notice who the Holy Spirit called and who the church affirmed? Was it just anyone? No, it was Barnabas and Saul. Don't miss the significance of this. These men were listed among the church's top leadership group. They were involved in significant leadership, shepherding, and teaching roles in the church.

The church did not send just anyone. Nor did the church ask for or wait until there were volunteers. They sent out two of their very best leaders and teachers. Why is this important? They sent out the men who had already proven themselves in the ministry and leadership of the church.[35] They were not the untested, the untried, or the unproven. They were not people with good intentions but no clear ministry track record. Instead, they sent out their very best people.

One more thing: who commissioned the missionaries? Verse 3 says, "Then after fasting and praying they [the church] laid their hands on them and sent them off." But in verse 4 it says, "So, being sent out by the Holy Spirit, they went down to Seleucia." There is a wonderful partnership pictured here. The Spirit sent them out by instructing the church to do so, and the church sent them, having been directed by the Spirit. This was not just the organizational program or agenda of the church; it was God's agenda. This was not merely a human endeavor; it was the work of the Holy Spirit through the church family. The church's ministry is not just about itself, but about the work of the Holy Spirit.

It would be important to notice that this passage illustrates a significant balance and provides a corrective between two extremes. The first extreme is the individualism we see when a person claims a call and guidance by the Spirit without any reference to or inclusion of the church family. A "call" is announced by the

---

[35] Let's not forget that a young man, Mark, also set out on the journey. The text tells us he went along to assist them. We are not told exactly what that meant, but we do know that partway through the journey, he left the team and returned home to Jerusalem. We are not told why because Luke simply announces it in 13:13 without placing blame. But in Acts 15:38 it becomes clear that Mark actually deserted them. Was he homesick, missing his mother and her large house and servants in Jerusalem? Did he resent the change in the leadership of the team from Barnabas to Paul? Did he disagree with Paul's bold policy of evangelizing the Gentiles? Did he struggle with fear of the difficult climb over the Taurus mountains, which were known to be infested with bandits? Did he disagree with Paul making the trip over the mountains because he was sick and Mark thought it was foolish for him to travel? We are not told, but the good news is that later, through the ongoing encouragement of Barnabas, he recovered and again became helpful to Paul (see Colossians 4:10 and 2 Timothy 4:11). Sometimes teams will have people like Mark, but the head and heart of the team must be our best people.

individual, and the church is asked to support it without question. Usually that support comes in the form of a request for finances. To make matters worse, there are missionary-sending agencies that do not include the local church in the discussion but will accept the candidate for service without reference from the church. The other extreme is institutionalism, where decision making is done by the church without reference to the Spirit and without much prayer or concern for God's leading. Decisions are made according to what seems financially expedient or best for the life of the church, with little regard for the sacrifice-demanding mandate to take the gospel to all nations.

Just before we leave Antioch and the newly formed missionary team, there is something else we need to take note of. Did you see what they did when they arrived at Salamis on Cyprus? The text says, "they proclaimed the word of God in the synagogues of the Jews" (Acts 13:5). Why is that significant? First, it tells us that they understood their primary task: to proclaim God's Word. This is why they were sent out, and this is what they did. Nothing was more important than this. Nothing! Second, by going to the synagogue, they demonstrate the missiological principle of reaching a community beginning with common ground.

Antioch and Us

Most tourists like to take a memento or souvenir home from the places they visit. So what is it we can take home from Antioch? How does the story of this church affect our own? There are a number of things. First, we need to prayerfully identify those whom the Holy Spirit is calling to carry the gospel to other nations. Jesus told us, "The harvest is plentiful, but the workers are few." He then called on us to "pray earnestly to the Lord of the harvest to send out laborers into his harvest" (Luke 10:2). The believers at Antioch prayed and fasted before commissioning the first missionaries. They wanted the guidance of the Lord of the harvest.

We need to also identify them by their giftedness, their godly character, their fruitful ministry experience, and their leadership skills. Mission work is not for the inexperienced, the untested, the spiritually immature, the untrained, or the timid. More pointedly, the first place we ought to look to identify those whom the Holy Spirit might be calling is the top levels of our leadership and ministry. This means we may need to get beyond ourselves and say farewell to our favorite leaders and teachers and preachers.

The following comes from a letter written in June 2011 by an African leader to churches in North America:

> "Please send us your adults, and not just your children. I realize that most career missionaries had a short-term experience that played a significant role in determining their future ministry—but I am troubled at the number of children you send our way for one- and two-week trips. Surely even in America there is a limit to how much money will be set aside for global missions, and this must be consuming an inordinately large amount of it. Please send us some people ready to learn our language and our culture, who can then live and work with us to help us educate and develop our church. Related to this—we really don't need construction workers from your region, as we have manual laborers of our own—nor do we need skits and songs in languages we don't understand and music we find interesting but foreign."[36]

Although we might have questions about some of the comments, the main point is well stated: send us your best people.

If someone declares an interest in missions, we need to make

[36] Borthwick, 2012, 206-207.

careful inquiry to clarify that call. Why do they think they are called? What are they called to do? Who else affirms their call? What does their current ministry activity look like, and how does it sustain a call to missions? What educational preparation have they undergone to prepare them for the task? What preparation are they willing to undergo to get ready? Do they understand the gospel and have a solid grasp of God's Word?

"Tragically, even among Christians with great enthusiasm for world mission, there is often not only profound ignorance of great vistas of biblical revelation, but even impatience with the prolonged effort that is needed to soak ourselves in these texts until our whole thinking and behaviour are shaped by the story they tell, the worldview that story generates, the demands it lays on us and the hope it sets before us. The attitude of some is that all you need is the Great Commission and the power of the Holy Spirit. Bible teaching or biblical theology will only serve to delay you in the urgent task."[37] The response of one "called" young man to the question about the need for biblical studies education as preparation for missions work was, "I don't have time and that stuff seems so simple and elementary to me." Is that the right response?

Since the primary task of missions is proclaiming the gospel, planting churches, and raising up the next generation of leaders who will carry the gospel in ever-widening circles, it demands serious preparation. Central to that preparation must be a thorough understanding of the Bible. Stott agrees when he writes:

> Let us not consume all our energies arguing about the Word of God; let's start using it. It will prove its divine origin by its divine power. Let's let it loose in the world! If only every Christian missionary and evangelist proclaimed the biblical gospel with faithfulness and sensitivity, and every Christian

---

[37] Wright, 2010, 39.

preacher were a faithful expositor of God's Word! Then God would display his saving power. Without the Bible world evangelization is impossible. For without the Bible we have not a gospel to take to the nations, nor warrant to take it to them, no idea of how to set about the task, and no hope of any success. It is the Bible that gives us the mandate, the message, the model and the power we need for world evangelization. So let's seek to repossess it by diligent study and meditation. Let's heed its summons, grasp its message, follow its directions and trust its power. Let's lift up our voices and make it known.[38]

"Not everyone has to have university degrees to be used by God, but don't cut your formal schooling short just because you suspect God is running out of time!"[39]

Second, when we identify those whom the Lord is calling, we need to challenge them to get beyond themselves and invest their lives in the cause of the gospel well beyond their comfort level. With that challenge, we must commit ourselves to preparing, commissioning, and sending them out with all the support they need to accomplish their God-given assignment.

Missionary Development Process

It would do us well to carefully think through and follow a detailed missionary development process. Typically individuals attend a missions event or conference and sense God's leading in their life. The next step they take is a conversation with one or more missions-sending agencies about opportunities for service. The formal

---

[38] Stott, 2009, 26.
[39] Hoke and Taylor, 2009, 743.

application process begins with the agency, and the church only officially finds out about the aspiring missionary when the agency asks for formal references or when the candidate announces they have been accepted by the mission. At this point it is very difficult to halt the forward momentum even though there might be concerns from the church's point of view. To question the new missionary or the mission agency causes a great deal of hurt, and the candidate withdraws from the process in disappointment, or angrily rejects the missions committee's recommendations and perhaps fades from the life of the church.

I remember well the history of a missionary candidate who was meeting with the missions committee early on in my tenure as a missions pastor. He had been accepted by the mission and was engaging the church in the conversation since it was time to seek the financial support of the church via the missions committee. As I listened to the conversation, I became convinced that he was not ready to embark on his overseas assignment, nor did I think we were ready to send him. I admit I stood at odds with some of the missions committee when I communicated my concerns, but we decided to ask him to get further preparation. It fell to me to communicate the decision to him, and his response was anger and hurt. After about four months of silence, he returned to the conversation and asked what he needed to get ready to go. We laid out a plan that included biblical studies courses and active ministry involvement. Two years later, we agreed he was ready to go. The collective response to our decision from both him and his mission leaders has been, "Taking the time for further preparation was the best thing that could have happened."

Although this story turned out well, many do not. But to alleviate these kinds of problems, the process toward long-term missions ministry should begin with a discussion at the local church level. The initial conversation should include a description and clarification of the person's "call." It should include questions about their ministry experience, giftedness, and biblical studies preparation.

Meeting time should be spent outlining the process the church wants to use to respond to the leading of the Lord, and include recommendations about sending agencies that work in the field of their call.[40] The potential missionary should do some research on the history of the region and what is currently happening in terms of gospel ministry.

At the local church level, the missionary-development process should also include a somewhat formal application document. In addition to basic family information, this application form should ask questions related to the person's health, finances, indebtedness, education, employment record, family relationships, conversion experience, spiritual growth disciplines, ministry participation, theological understandings, future plans for preparation and ministry, and references from various venues of their life. This type of formal application indicates to the candidate the seriousness and significance of the ministry they wish to enter into.

Only upon the review and approval of the application to the church should the candidate begin the application process with the sending agency. This will give them significant confidence as

---

[40] As an addendum to this point, it would be important that members of the local church take time to think about which agencies they can partner with comfortably. Ideally these sending agencies will share the local church's same theological framework and missions priorities. They should also value the active participation of the local church in the recruitment, preparation, and accountability of missionaries serving with them. A good indication of this is the point and level of decision making at which they engage the local church in the application process.

When a sending agency is approved as a partner organization, under the direction of their leaders and when possible, the church should promote the organization within the local church; assist in recruiting workers for the organization from among the church family; partner with the organization in short-term ministry opportunities by providing qualified teams or individuals who will enhance and accelerate the on-ground ministries; and partner with the organization to accomplish specific long-term projects through financial resources, people, and materials.

they enter into the conversations they will have with the agency, knowing their church is working with them and encouraging them to proceed. The church will want to be in direct contact with the sending agency so that by the time the candidate is approved, a strong relationship will already have been formed between church and agency. This relationship will form the basis of designing any necessary further preparation as well as building a foundation for mutual accountability and the ongoing care and support of the missionary.

More than Money and Prayer

Sending, however, means more than money and prayer. These by no means make up the total picture. Along with those who go, those who send need to get beyond themselves. In 3 John 6–8, John writes these words to Gaius: "Beloved, it is a faithful thing you do in all your efforts for these brothers, strangers as they are, who testified to your love before the church. You will do well to send them on their journey in a manner worthy of God. For they have gone out for the sake of the name, accepting nothing from the Gentiles. Therefore, we ought to support people like these, that we may be fellow workers for the truth." To "send them on their journey," Christopher J. H. Wright says, "meant more than waving good-bye. The verb *propempo* is almost a technical term elsewhere in the New Testament for making all the necessary arrangements and provisions for someone's journey (Acts 15:3; 21:5; Rom. 15:24; 1 Cor. 16:6, 10–11; 2 Cor. 1:16; Titus 3:13). It would include providing food, money for fares or overnight accommodation, perhaps companions for safety, and letters of introduction or commendation for those at the other end."[41]

Notice as well how Gaius was instructed to send them—"in a manner worthy of God." That means in a way that would be

---

[41] Wright, 2010, 219.

approved by God or in the same way we would send Jesus himself. Missionaries are sent out in the same work of world evangelism to which the Lord was sent, and for which he gave his life.

It is not enough to pray "Bless the missionary" prayers and send a token amount of money each month. We need to move far beyond that. "Prayer and giving are obvious ways to support mission enterprise. But when people focus their lives on fulfilling the total global task and apply their experience and gifts in creative ways to seeing particular mission efforts advance, they make surprisingly significant contributions."[42] Sending includes words of encouragement, remembering special days, and expensive telephone calls. It may mean paying your own way to spend a few days encouraging them on the field, or bringing them home to spend time with their family for a special occasion, or sending them on a refreshing vacation break. It means sacrificial care when the missionary returns home that might include a ride from the airport, a place to stay, a car to drive, and a cell phone plan to use. It includes using skills and training to provide communication tools, fix computers, create websites, and publish materials. It includes the provision of dental care and a medical checkup when health care funding is inadequate. It means going out of the routine of normal life to take the initiative to provide a cup of coffee, share a meal, or buy a book or an e-reader before they ask.

Yes, missionaries need your prayer and financial support, but they also need you to build into their lives and show that you love them. They need to know that what they do is important enough to you that you too are willing to sacrifice for the cause of the gospel and the glory of God. Such beyond-ourselves sending, as John tells Gaius, makes us "fellow workers for the truth." As John Piper very pointedly says, "There are only three kinds of people in relation to missions: Goers, Senders, and Disobedient."[43]

---

[42] Hickman, Hawthorne and Ahrend, 2009, 727.

[43] Piper, October 25, 2009.

Summarizing the Principles

1. Missionary ministry does not begin overseas, but at home in the context of a local church and its ministry.

2. The missionary call is not just an individual event but ought to include the local church and its leadership.

3. We need to send our best out on missionary assignments, and if they are not our best, we need to do all we can to help them become our best.

4. Because the primary task of the missionary is the proclamation of the Word of God, a thorough biblical education is one of the most important aspects of missionary preparation.

5. We must commit ourselves to preparing, commissioning and sending missionaries out with all the support they need to accomplish their God-given assignment.

6. We need to establish a clear missionary development process that can be used to guide candidates toward effective ministry.

7. Sending needs to be as sacrificial as going.

Questions to Consider

1. How might your church intentionally challenge and recruit effective ministry leaders to consider overseas missions? If you were to make a list of your best possible missionary candidates, who would be on that list? What challenges would your church face in sending them?

2. How much consideration does your church give to the necessity of a strong biblical education for missionary

candidates? What can or should you as a church do to raise the standard for potential missionaries?

3. What does the missionary-development process look like in your church? If there isn't a clear process, what do you think needs to be a part of that process, and in what order should the steps take place?

4. What are you doing beyond giving and prayer to support your missionaries? What can you do to let them know you are going beyond yourself and also sacrificing for the cause of the gospel?

— Chapter 6 —

By Serving in Ministry Partnerships

S erving is hard. It seems so much easier to be in charge. A servant has to do the difficult stuff, the dirty stuff, the unglamorous stuff. The leader gets to do the important stuff like making decisions and directing others. The servant gets their hands dirty while the leader gets to wear the nice clothes. The servant works behind the scenes while the leader gets the spotlight and the attention and the praise.

Who Is the Greatest?

Whether we are actually leaders or not, there is a bit of the leader mentality in all of us. The disciples' struggle with this was exposed in their discussion of who would be the greatest in the coming kingdom of God. It is easy to write them off as being immature like children who are fighting about who is better or whose father is bigger and stronger. But before we do that, we need to take a look into our own hearts. We all want recognition. We all want to be noticed as significant. We all want to accomplish something great. We all want to be praised. This is not all bad, but when it gets perverted, it becomes a problem. To settle the debate between the disciples, Jesus "said to them, 'If anyone would be first, he must be last of all and servant of all.' And he took a child and put him in the midst of them, and taking him in his arms, he said to them, 'Whoever receives one such child in my name receives me, and whoever receives me, receives not me but him who sent me" (Mark 9:35–37). Luke adds, "For he who is least among you all is the one who is great" (Luke 9:45).

Jesus recognizes that the desire to be great, to accomplish something of value is a good thing. He created us to be great and to be significant. When we come to the end of our lives, he wants us to have invested our lives well and to have accomplished something noteworthy and lasting for his glory. Although he does not condemn the desire to be great, he does recognize that too often we pervert that desire. It becomes corrupt when it moves from being a desire to be great to a desire to be recognized as great. It gets perverted when it becomes a desire to be measured and seen as greater than someone else. It gets bent when our desire is all about ourselves.

Jesus also gives us a way to redeem our desire to do great things. "He says true greatness is not wanting to be first while others are second and third and fourth, but true greatness is the willingness to be last. And true greatness is not positioning yourself so that others praise you, but true greatness is putting yourself in a position to serve everyone—to be a blessing to as many as you possibly can."[44] To illustrate this even further Jesus takes a child into his arms and tells his disciples that greatness comes by serving the smallest and most insignificant. The child represents those who have little say in the world, those who cannot pay us back for our service, those who don't have a lot of influence on our status, those who will not tell others how great we might be. Serving people like this proves whether you want to accomplish great things or be thought of by others as great. Serving people like this reveals whether your life is about your recognition or whether you have gotten beyond yourself.

---

[44] Piper, February 23, 1992.

What has this got to do with ministry partnerships? Everything! Our typical North American tendency is to go and do and come back and tell what great people we are. We love to go and lead, to be seen, to be heard, to be recognized. We love to introduce our ideas and plans and programs. We love it when others admire us and what we have accomplished. We love to tell all the great things we have done. We are not very good at serving in the quiet, unknown, unannounced places of ministry.

I had the privilege of spending a few days with a man who gives leadership to a massive church-planting movement along the Amazon River. This man is small and quiet, but has substantial influence in the lives and ministry of hundreds of indigenous church planters. Our church was partnering with one of the church plants by providing physical labor for the construction of a new building. One particular day I returned to the boat we were staying on to get something I had forgotten to take to the worksite. As I made my way through the boat I noticed this leader of leaders doing something shocking. He was cleaning the toilets that were used by the boat's crew as well as our construction team of eight. I think he was somewhat embarrassed that I saw him doing it, but later I found out that he had adopted this as his responsibility whenever he takes a team out on the river.

That is servanthood! And, that is the same kind of servanthood we need to bring to the table of ministry partnerships. We don't need to go as leaders. We don't need to be in charge. We don't have to do things our way. But we need to go as servants. And our servanthood must begin with a humility that listens.

Founded by evangelist Bob Schindler in 1991, Mission ONE has become a leading ministry whose key strategy for world evangelization is building partnerships with indigenous ministries. Mission ONE mobilizes and trains people of the church for partnership with national missionaries, focusing on unreached people groups, and serving the poor and oppressed. In their partnership agreement form they write the following: "The foundation for healthy partnerships is following humbly our Lord Jesus Christ, for the glory of God. Humility is at the core of a healthy partnership. Leaders of mission agencies engaged in healthy partnerships are characterized by humility. We believe that this one thing—Christlike humility—will more than anything else determine the long-term health of a cross-cultural partnership. One of the best ways to express humility is by listening. Listening carefully to one another, listening with our hearts, is a vital part of developing trust and keeping trust—and for building a long successful partnership."[45]

The Changing World

In his book *Western Christians in Global Ministry,* Paul Borthwick reminds us that "Even though the Western world has dominated Christianity for much of Christian history, Christianity is now primarily a nonwhite, non-Western, nonwealthy religion."[46] We as North Americans are no longer at the center of the history of missions. The shift has moved toward what is called the Global South, where there are now more believers than there are in the Global North. True Christianity has grown by more than 300 million believers in the past ten years. Ten million of those were from North America and Europe, and 290 million were from developing countries such as Nigeria, Brazil, India, and China. In 1800, 99 percent of the believers in the world lived in Europe and North America, with only 1 percent being in all of Latin America, Africa, and Asia combined. By 1985 the percentage was 50/50. In 2010 it was reported that 31 percent of believers were from Europe and North America, and 69 percent were from Latin America, Africa, and Asia.[47] Exact numbers are hard to come by, but on a 2013 trip to Cuba I learned that about 20 percent of the 2 million people who

---

[45] Mischke, 2013.

[46] Borthwick, 2012, 36.

[47] Signs of the Times, Great Commission Powerpoints. 2013.

live in Havana attend church on Sunday. In China, we are told, there are estimates of 80 to 120 million believers. Among the 83 million people in Egypt, it is estimated there are 3 million believers. On and on the list could go. We ought to rejoice in these numbers because they represent the fruit of earlier missionaries who invested their lives in the cause of the gospel, often at great personal cost. Though there are debates about their ministry methods, and though their history is tainted with mistakes, the abuse of power, and cultural superiority, God has been at work through their lives, just as he promised. He has been building his church.

It used to be that missions were primarily "from the West to the rest." That meant that most mission activity originated in Western countries whose churches sent our workers to share the gospel with those in the east or south. But today much of that has changed. *Missions* is more correctly defined as "from anywhere to everywhere." The largest missionary-sending countries are no longer the United Kingdom, the United States, and Canada. Now among the most prolific sending countries are Korea, Brazil, and the Philippines. In Brazil alone, more than 100 mission agencies have emerged, sending more than 2,000 Brazilian missionaries to eighty-five countries. Reports in 2013 placed the number of Korean missionaries worldwide at around 18,000—spread across 168 countries. Sub-Saharan Africa is becoming a sending base for missionaries to Islamic North Africa.

Over the next fifteen to twenty years, it is estimated that those being sent out as missionaries will originate from the following countries:

- Korea—30,000
- China—50,000
- Philippines—10,000
- Nigeria—15,000
- India—40,000
- Latin America—21,000

Those once unreached are now becoming senders, leaving us with questions about our ongoing role. Where do we fit into this changing scene? What is our role? What do we bring to the missions table? What should we bring? These questions have led to a great debate.

The Great Debate

Over the past several years there has been a growing discussion on the role of North Americans in the completion of the Great Commission. As a strong voice in this debate, K. P. Yohannan says,

We are living in an age when over half the world's population—and the majority of the unreached people—live in countries that restrict Western missionaries. Thus, for the Western church today, priority number one must no longer be *going* but rather must be *sending*. Priority number two, then, should be *going as servants* to train and assist our brothers and sisters in finishing this final task.[48]

Yohannan calls on North American churches to focus their resource investment in sending out the nearest indigenous workers rather than sending out North American workers. His reasoning is that the indigenous worker will have a shorter cultural adjustment period, learn a local dialect quicker and require far less funding than the North American who comes with all of the cost of their safety networks.

To illustrate his point he writes:

> According to a study by a conservative missions board in the Philippines, an American couple needed an annual budget of $2,400 for language training, $720 for support-raising "prayer letters," $1,200 for contingencies, $2,100 for insurance and Social Security and $1,500 for furlough fund,

---

[48] Yohannan, 2004, 53.

making a total of $7,920. None of this is needed by the indigenous missionary.

Other comparisons are quite revealing. The American couple would need $6,000 for field work expenses; the Filipinos, only $132. Miscellaneous costs for the Americans would total $1,200; for the Filipinos, $67. A car for the Americans would cost $3,000 annually, amortized over five years; for the Filipinos, only $67 would be needed for jeepney fares. Housing costs for the American couple would total $4,800; for the Filipinos, $267. Personal family needs for the American would be $7,200, as opposed to $667 for the Filipino missionaries.[49]

Added to this, Sherwood Lingenfelter is quoted as saying,

While most middle-class families would not hesitate to spend four hundred dollars a month on a car payment, two or three hundred dollars on credit card purchases, and another two or three hundred on cell phone, cable television and internet access, they do not comprehend that they could fully support seven Indian missionaries or trainers of trainers with those same dollars. The opportunity and challenge for the western church is to invest in the equipping of leaders in India, Africa, and the poorest nations of Asia. The opportunity is vast, and the needs are critical. The Lord is waiting for the rich to partner with the poor to make disciples of the nations.[50]

[49] Ibid., 156-157.
[50] Lingenfelter in AM Quotes, 2013.

But does this mean we should abandon sending out missionaries from our churches?

In responding to the changes that have come with the expansion of the gospel in the global south, Piper puts it better than anyone else:

> This is a great cause for Christians to rejoice in the sovereign grace of God. But what it does not mean is that the day of sending missionaries from our churches in the West is over. That would be a tragic misunderstanding of the situation. Partnership in mission with the Global South does not mean that all the unreached peoples of the world can be reached by people who are in the Global South. Don't buy into the idea that we should send our money, not our people. That would sound very much like: "Let them shed their blood, not ours; we'll just send money."
>
> Many people have embraced the uninformed notion that it is always more efficient and culturally effective to support ministries in the Global South to do the work of missions rather than pay tens of thousands of dollars each year to send Western workers.
>
> But it is both-and, not either-or. It is uninformed, indeed misinformed, to assume that local churches or nearby missionaries in the Global South can always reach an unreached people better than Western workers can.
>
> It is uninformed, first of all, because in pioneer, frontier missionary situations, there are no local churches to do the work. That's the meaning of being an unreached people. And secondly, there is no assurance that being within five hundred miles

of an unreached people makes you more effective in learning their language, and crossing their culture, and loving them, and teaching the truth. This is especially true if there are old tribal hostilities to be overcome in the local region. Such a strategy may sometimes be best; other times not.

The day of Western missions is not over. It never will be over until Jesus comes. There are many ways to partner with believers around the world, besides simply sending money. And we will be servants, not masters, in those relationships.[51]

This debate need not result in an either/or conclusion. I believe it is a both/and. It would be wise to consider where and when and with whom to invest in indigenous workers. But it is also important to acknowledge that the "go" of the Great Commission has not been withdrawn from the churches in the West. From "everywhere to everywhere" still involves us. A balanced missions portfolio will have both.

The previous chapter dealt with the support of our own long-term missionaries, but what are the appropriate criteria for partnering with and supporting indigenous workers? Let me suggest the following in the form of questions:

- What are their theological foundations? How do they align with yours?
- What is the purpose of their work? Are they actually proclaiming the gospel? Are churches being planted? Are biblical leaders being trained?
- What are their accountability structures, both for the use of their finances and for task accomplishment?

---

[51] Piper, October 25, 2009.

- What are their connections with the tax structure of your country that allow you to give tax-deductible donations to them?
- What type of reporting is available to your church? Are you comfortable with the content and frequency of those reports?
- How long will your commitment to them endure? Are you in it for only a season or for the long haul?
- Will you be fully supporting an indigenous worker or will you be partnering with others in their support? (The value of the shared support is that fluctuations in the commitments of churches or individuals will not leave an indigenous worker without any support.)
- What percentage of overhead is taken by the organization before the funds reach the indigenous worker? Are you happy with that amount?

What Is Our Role in Partnerships?

As the world of missions continues to change, so does the view that the local church plays in missions work. It used to be that a church's involvement in missions was largely confined to providing financial and prayer support to missionaries who went out under the banner of various missions agencies. The missionary would go for a term and return on furlough for a rest and to report on their ministry in person. Between their trips home they would write prayer letters to remind their supporters of their lives and work. But today, with digital communication and increased travel opportunities, things are changing. Many churches are moving away from working in missions at arm's length and becoming increasingly involved both in the recruitment process and the ongoing field ministry. There is a desire to become personally involved and more in touch with missions. With this desire comes the need to build partnerships to facilitate it.

Traditionally we have supported our own long-term workers. Now we have opportunities to support indigenous workers. But is there a role for us beyond that? If so, what is it? What else do we bring to the table? What has God blessed us with that becomes a resource to the nations? If we were to do inventory, we might find we have a lot to put on the table. We have greater financial resources, greater freedom to travel, greater education systems, and greater access to scholastic materials. We have a great deal to offer. But, do we really? We actually have little to offer if we do not get beyond ourselves.

Because we live in the wealth of the West, because we have highly developed systems of government, education, health care, digital communication, and transportation, it is very easy to see ourselves as masters and not servants. Our task-driven orientation and pride in our perfected structures pushes us to export them elsewhere. Just examine the last few years in the Middle East and our attempts to export and impose our form of democracy on other nations. The record does not speak well of that kind of venture. For example, Lara Jakes in the Huffington Post writes of the failure of the US State Department and the waste of more than $200 million on a program to train Iraqi police that Baghdad says is neither needed nor wanted:

> The Police Development Program—which was drawn up to be the single largest State Department program in the world—was envisioned as a five-year, multibillion-dollar push to train security forces after the U.S. military left last December. But Iraqi political leaders, anxious to keep their distance from the Americans, were unenthusiastic. A report by the Special Inspector General for Iraq Reconstruction, released Monday, found that the American Embassy in Baghdad never got a written commitment from Iraq to participate. Now, facing

what the report called Baghdad's "disinterest" in
the project, the embassy is gutting what was supposed to be the centerpiece of ongoing U.S. training
efforts in Iraq. "A major lesson learned from Iraq
is that host country buy-in to proposed programs
is essential to the long-term success of relief and
reconstruction activities. The Police Development
Program experience powerfully underscores that
point," auditors wrote in a 41-page summary of
their inspection.[52]

This is not just an isolated story of the US government, but a
story that could be repeated again and again by missionaries and
agencies who have sought to export themselves into another part
of the world without regard for cultural differences.

The place to begin in building partnerships is not with what we
have, but with what they need. This is a very hard lesson to learn.
I remember too well sitting on my side of the ocean designing a
biblical studies training system for use in the Middle East. I had it all
nicely mapped out, until I actually went to the Middle East. There
I learned that my PhD in Christian education didn't mean I really
knew what I was doing. I had designed something that I thought
would work, but soon found I needed to get beyond myself and
abandon my ideas and start over. The Lord very graciously brought
people and circumstances into my life who helped me see that I
couldn't just export my program. I needed to participate in many
conversations to learn and then redesign in cooperation with the
people and culture in which the program would operate. I needed
to first go as a servant, rather than as the master.

We need to get beyond ourselves and include our overseas
partners in the design, development. and implementation of the
ministry rather than impose our blueprints on them. In their book

---

[52] Jakes, 2012.

When Helping Hurts, Fikkert and Corbett tell this repeated-all-too-often story:

> Wanting to assist a village in Columbia with its rice production, a nonprofit organization gathered the villagers into a cooperative and bought them a thresher, a motorized huller, a generator, and a tractor. Rice production boomed, and the cooperative sold the rice at the highest price the farmers had ever received. The nonprofit organization then left the village, but several years later one of its staff members returned to find that the cooperative had completely disbanded and that all of the equipment was broken down and rusting away in the fields. In fact, some of the equipment had never been used at all. Yet, as the staff member walked through the village, the people pleaded with him, "If [your organization] would just come help us again, we could do so much!"[53]

The problem was not the equipment or the reason behind it. The problem was that the solution came independent of the community. There was inadequate participation of the community in the process. Everything worked as long as the Westerns were there, but with their withdrawal came the disintegration of the imposed program. "Although the blueprint approach *appears* to be very efficient, it often fails because it imposes solutions on poor communities that are inconsistent with local culture, that are not embraced or 'owned' by the community members, or that cannot work in a particular setting."[54]

We need to get beyond ourselves by letting others give to us.

[53] Corbett and Fickkert, 2009, 141.
[54] Ibid., 142.

We live in a world where we are taught to be independent and self-sufficient. We build our lives around the attainment of our goals and the acquiring of stuff that will bring us comfort and control. As a result, it is hard to receive something from someone else. It is hard for us to be the recipient of someone else's support. But true partnership involves giving and receiving. "Every partner must bring resources to the table. If all parties do not bring resources, it is not a *partnership*; it is *ownership*, and there will be controlling dynamics from the side of the owner. The Western church must begin to intentionally develop patterns where both partners state their purpose for coming together, the vision they would like to employ. Then, together they can determine the total resources they need to accomplish the combined objectives of the partnership, and clearly decide who is bringing what to the table."[55] Too often we place ourselves as the great benefactor whose task it is to give to others.

On one of our trips to Mali, my wife and I had the delight of sharing Christmas Day with a small local church. As the church family gathered under the rusty tin roof, they were dressed in their finest. The ladies wore their colorful dresses, and the men's shirts were pressed with creases that made them look as if they had just come out of the packaging. After the service we were invited across the dusty yard to the pastor's home for lunch. The kitchen was an outdoor fire surrounded by rocks on which sat the various pans and cooking utensils. The only indoor part of the home was the sleeping rooms. The living room consisted of a thatched roof and plastic chairs. As we sat and visited together, chickens pecked the ground near our feet. When the meal was served, we moved our chairs closer together and with our hands began eating from the common pot. This was the most unique Christmas celebration we had ever experienced. At the conclusion of the meal, one of the old men, an elder in the church, brought me a gift as an expression

---

[55] Adeney, 2009, 257-258.

of thanksgiving for coming and speaking that morning. It was a huge gift by their standards. In fact, this was proportionately one of the largest honorariums I have ever received for speaking. The gift: a live chicken.

Did I need a live chicken? Did I want a live chicken? No, I didn't even know what to do with it. But that day I realized that I was not the only one who was a giver. I was also a receiver, and I need to be a humble recipient of the gifts of others. Ministry partnership is a two-way path, and I need to be as much a receiver as a giver.

It may be a humbling experience, but one way to be a recipient and not just a giver is to allow those you visit overseas to provide your housing and food. In our individualism it feels much better to stay at a hotel and eat our choice of food in a restaurant. I like my own space and freedom to make my own food choices. But that does not happen when you surrender yourself to their hospitality. You will end up sleeping in all kinds of places and eating all kinds of food. But you will also give them an opportunity to care for you.

We need to get beyond ourselves by not seeing ourselves as the only initiators or controllers of ministry. We do not have to be the ones with the ideas and initiative. We need to find out what the Lord is doing through various people and organizations and join with them. We may have necessary boundaries in terms of whom and what we will partner with, but let's not always think we have to be the ones who start and control everything. Borthwick writes about the effect of letting others be in charge:

> Letting go of the controls for us has meant joining our partners in ministry without knowing the daily schedule, without knowing exactly where we are staying, without knowing who will meet us at the airport and without knowing what we will eat. Add to all this the complexity of not knowing local languages, and the feelings of powerlessness expand. One of our slogans is this: "Building

crosscultural relationships is easier if we accept the
fact that 40 percent of the time we will have no idea
what's going on." In these situations, however, our
reliance on God and our dependence on our global
colleagues increases, creating greater opportunities for us to be on the receiving end of their care.[56]

We need to get beyond ourselves by building partnerships
around relationships and not just finances. The topic of money is
where we tend to go right away. One of the early questions we ask
is "How much do you need?" But when we start there and build
our partnership there, it is very easy for us to assess the partnership
only around measurable financial gain. The partnership is seen as
a contract with decisions about ongoing support made through
annual budget calculations and considerations. One of the lessons
I am learning from our brothers in the Middle East is that our
relationship with them is more important than the finances we
send them. The question I get asked continually is, "When are you
coming to see us?" and not "When are you sending the money?"
To them, our partnership is about relationship. It is not a business
contract. In fact, long after we have accomplished our part of the
ministry partnership, it is expected that the relationship will continue and that personal contact will carry on far beyond the terms
of the partnership.

We need to get beyond ourselves by freely offering our resources
to others. As the Western church, we have had the freedom and the
means to develop a lot of great resources. Some are not as useful
cross-culturally as others, but we are in the kingdom business and
not in the publishing business. We are in the business of declaring
the message of God's grace and not in the business of building our
own kingdoms with our names on them. We need to be generous
in the distribution of that which God has entrusted to us.

[56] Borthwick, 2012, 133.

I was sitting in the office of a denominational leader in Havana and participating in a discussion about a ministry partnership. As the Cuban leader was sharing the extent of their ministry, I thought to myself, *Why am I here?* After a few minutes, I verbalized my question with these words: "Why do you need us? It seems that you already have a great ministry." His response was, "God has brought you here and you cannot leave this room." In my wild imagination I quickly reminded myself of the country I was in and wondered if I was going to be the victim of some kind of political situation. But before I could pursue that crazy line of thinking, he said something like this: "We have examined a lot of training programs and have had lots of people come to our country trying to bring their program to us. But your church has what we need, and you are offering it to us without a list of demands or conditions. You are giving us the resources and asking us to give leadership to the decisions of implementation. This is the kind of group we can build true ministry partnerships with."

Part of me rejoices in what he said, but part of me cringes. When I allow my administrative, task-oriented, controlling mind think to of all the "what if" implications of giving something away, I wince. But then I am taken back to these words of Jesus to his disciples: "You know that those who are considered rulers of the Gentiles lord it over them, and their great ones exercise authority over them. But it shall not be so among you. But whoever would be great among you must be your servant, and whoever would be first among you must be slave of all" (Mark 10:42–44). And if that was not enough, Jesus added the real kicker: "For even the Son of Man came not to be served but to serve, and to give his life as a ransom for many." It is those last words that remind me of our purpose in missions. It is those last words that drive us to the cross, where we picture what it means to serve. It is those words that motivate me to give up my need to always be in charge.

Summarizing the Principles

1. Although many of us like to lead, the core of ministry must be servanthood.
2. The center of the Christian world is shifting southward with more believers now living in the Global South than in the Global North.
3. With the shift to the south, missions has changed from the "West to the rest" to "from everywhere to anywhere."
4. We need to have a missions portfolio that has a balance between sending our own long-term workers and supporting indigenous workers.
5. Our role in missions partnerships must change from being leaders to being servants.

Questions to Consider

1. What ministry partnerships are you or your church involved in? How are decisions made by the partners?
2. Does your side of a ministry partnership look more like leadership than servanthood? In what ways can you become better servants to your overseas partners?
3. What does your church's missions portfolio look like? Do you support your own missionaries as well as indigenous workers?
4. What changes might help your church bring more balance to your missions program?

— Chapter 7 —
By Sending Prepared Short-Term Workers

While sitting in a café in Katmandu, I asked a veteran missionary about short-term missions work. She jumped at the chance to unload her frustrations with what she saw, in her opinion, was too often a waste of time and money. Members of one particular team that had recently visited their city had barely gotten into the van for the drive from the airport to the guest house when she was asked, "When do we get to go shopping?"

This was absolutely the wrong question! Yet it and similar questions get asked over and over again by those who venture from home on short-term missions trips. These trips have typically been made up of teams of high school and college-age students who enthusiastically set out from their home church to some far corner of the world to embark on a one- or two-week adventure in missions. The purpose for many of these adventures is just that—adventure. It is an opportunity to explore the world and to learn something of yourself as you typically "help" some poor people with something they need.

Jacqueline Salmon, in a Washington Post article on mission trips wrote, "From a few hundred in the 1960s, the trips have proliferated in recent years. A Princeton University study found that 1.6 million people took short-term mission trips—an average of eight days—in 2005. Estimates of the money spent on these trips are upwards of $2.4 billion a year. Vacation destinations are especially popular: Recent research has found that the Bahamas receives one short-term missionary for every 15 residents."[57]

The Bahamas? Sign me up. Especially when we can escape the cold of the north and have an adventure while someone else pays for it. Or how about Mexico? Here is an all-too-typical excerpt from a church bulletin about an upcoming mission trip to Mexico:

> [Our congregation] is sponsoring a women's-only mission trip to beautiful Guadalajara, Mexico! We'll spend the week of June 11–18 in Guadalajara (also known as the shopping capital of Mexico), where we will have the incredible opportunity to minister to, pray for, and teach women in a vibrant church community. And this trip isn't a "rough-roach-in-your-bed" kind of experience either— we'll be housed in nice clean hotel rooms, eat lots of salsa, and have plenty of time to shop! Our hope is to take at least fifteen women (including teenage daughters) on this Mexican Ministry Outreach ... We trust that God will expand our hearts for Him as He expands our ministry to the women of Guadalajara. If you are remotely interested in this adventure—or if you're just in the mood for Mexico after all this winter weather—call for more details about this fantastic outreach opportunity.[58]

It is no wonder critics scornfully call such trips "religious tourism" undertaken by "vacationaries". If this is short-term missions, I think we have a problem.

One of the ways we sell each other on the value of short-term

---

[57] Salmon, 2008.
[58] Livermore, 2006, 52.

missions is by proclaiming their value in the life of the participant. We tell each other that joining a short-term team will have a huge effect on our life. It will change the way we look at the world. It will change the way we spend money. It will give us a new enthusiasm about sharing Christ at home, and it will change the way we think about and support missions. But does it? "Some studies demonstrate that while participants come home with lofty aspirations of buying less, praying more, and sharing Christ more, within six to eight weeks, most resort back to all the same assumptions and behaviors they had prior to the trip."[59]

Unfortunately this is not our only problem. There's more. Too much more. How about the view we sometimes have of ourselves as being God's gift to the places we visit? What about our perspective on how effective we are in what we are doing while we are there? As one writer said, "Imagine how we in America would feel if people from another country—like Germany or Korea—came to our church and took over our Summer Vacation Bible School, asking us to serve as their interpreters because they did not speak our language. What if the illustrations they gave our children about how to live were, for the most part, culturally irrelevant? And how would we feel if while these foreigners were with us, they dominated our schedule and made it difficult for us to get our work done. Sadly, this is often the impact of poorly planned short-term mission trips."[60]

What about the sacrifices that are made by short-term missionaries? After all, these people leave the comfort of home to endure rigorous travel, sleep in different beds, eat different food, and experience different weather. That ought to count for something.

Yet Borthwick has a different take on this very attitude:

---

[59] Ver Beek, 2008.
[60] Schwartz, 2003.

> Too often, we who go to serve on cross-cultural short-term missions practice self-congratulatory servanthood. We live in the hut, eat the local food, endure the heat, and use the squat toilet, all the time quietly congratulating ourselves on our willingness to serve. The irony is this: I might be feeling proud as I 'sacrifice' my North American comforts to be with my Majority World family, but they don't necessarily see me as a servant. They welcome me as a guest, but to them, I am just living the way they do every day, fifty-two weeks a year. I am not acting as a servant; I am simply a new member of their family.[61]

Many times I have sat in contexts where I have had the privilege of hearing brothers and sisters share the cost of following Christ and taking the gospel to their own people. As I listened, I felt like a cheater. I used to think I knew what it meant to sacrifice until I heard them. The greatest sacrifice I probably have is to put a portion of my income into the offering each month. While in Thailand, I heard brothers from a neighboring country tell of the horrendous sacrifices they made for the cause of the gospel. I will never forget the words of one of the brothers as he stood to lead us in worship: "They can arrest us. They can throw us in prison. They can torture us and they can shoot us. But they can never make us stop worshipping Jesus Christ our Lord!" How little do we know about sacrifice!

Then there is the whole missionary construction-project enterprise. We often go to these places and export our expertise in building. We too often take the view that we know how to do it better and faster and more efficiently. Instead of going as learners, we want to go as teachers and instruct others how to do it right. Schwartz tells the story of a team of young Americans

---

[61] Borthwick, 2012, 122.

and Canadians who went to Zimbabwe on a six-week ministry trip where they would work alongside the Africans on a building project. After four weeks the team left for home. When asked what happened, the local African builder in charge of the project gave this explanation: "What the Americans didn't know is that we here in Africa also know how to build buildings. It isn't that they didn't work hard. The trowel was too slow to put mortar between the bricks, so they used their bare hands to speed things up. But they must remember that we built buildings before they came, and we will build buildings after they leave. Unfortunately, while they were here, they thought they were the only ones who knew how to build buildings. Finally things got so bad, we had to ask them to leave."[62]

There are a myriad of stories similar to this. "Some blunders include a wall built on the children's soccer field at an orphanage in Brazil that had to be torn down after the visitors left. In Mexico, a church was painted six times during one summer by six different groups. In Ecuador, a church was built but never used because the community said it was not needed."[63] But do these kinds of stories and problems mean we should abandon short-term mission trips? I don't think so, but they should cause us to examine what we are doing and take steps to get beyond ourselves to minimize the problems and maximize the positive effects. "If [the trips] are only about ourselves, then we're doing nothing more than using another culture ... to get some benefit at their expense," said the Reverend Roger Peterson, chairman of the Alliance for Excellence in Short-Term Mission ... "I don't care what verse of the Bible you read, it's wrong, it's wrong, it's wrong."[64]

---

[62] Schwartz, 2003.
[63] Salmon, 2008.
[64] Ibid.

Standards of Excellence

How do we get beyond ourselves so that we can do it right, or at least do it better? In answer to this question a host of responses can be garnered from seasoned missionaries as well as experienced short-term mission leaders. Hundreds of books and articles have been written about short-term ministry, and suggestions abound from many corners. Standards of Excellence in Short-Term Mission is an organization that provides a foundation for getting beyond ourselves. They have developed what they call 7 Standards that provide a starting place and framework for guiding short-term missions trips. These standards consist of the following:

1. God-Centeredness. An excellent short-term mission seeks first God's glory and his kingdom, and is expressed through our
    *   purpose—centering on God's glory and his ends throughout our entire STM process;
    *   lives—sound biblical doctrine, persistent prayer, and godliness in all our thoughts, words, and deeds;
    *   methods—wise, biblical, and culturally appropriate methods that bear spiritual fruit.
2. Empowering Partnerships. An excellent short-term mission establishes healthy, interdependent, ongoing relationships between sending and receiving partners, and is expressed by
    *   primary focus on intended receptors,
    *   plans that benefit all participants, and
    *   mutual trust and accountability.
3. Mutual Design. An excellent short-term mission collaboratively plans each specific outreach for the benefit of all participants, and is expressed by
    *   on-field methods and activities aligned to long-term strategies of the partnership,

- goer-guests' ability to implement their part of the plan, and
- host receivers' ability to implement their part of the plan.

4. Comprehensive Administration. An excellent short-term mission exhibits integrity through reliable setup and thorough administration for all participants, and is expressed by
   - truthfulness in promotion, finances, and reporting results;
   - appropriate risk management; and
   - quality program delivery and support logistics.

5. Qualified Leadership. An excellent short-term mission screens, trains, and develops capable leadership for all participants, and is expressed by
   - character—spiritually mature servant leadership;
   - skills—prepared, competent, organized, and accountable leadership; and
   - values—empowering and equipping leadership.

6. Appropriate Training. An excellent short-term mission prepares and equips all participants for the mutually designed outreach, and is expressed by
   - biblical, appropriate, and timely training;
   - ongoing training and equipping (pre-field, on-field, post-field); and
   - qualified trainers.

7. Thorough Follow-Through. An excellent short-term mission assures evaluation, debriefing, and appropriate follow-through for all participants, and is expressed by
   - comprehensive debriefing of all participants (pre-field, on-field, post-field);
   - thoughtful and appropriate follow-through for goer-guests; and
   - on-field and post-field evaluation among sending and receiving partners.

This all sounds good, but what does this look like in the local church setting? How do we make this work?

When, Where, and Why

First, the church needs to make some decision about the when, where, and why of short-term teams. It is not enough to send out teams because it is a cool idea or there is a unique opportunity. We have found that the most effective use of short-term teams is in connection with our long-term missionaries or projects. Our desire is to be a resource for the ongoing ministries we already support. Each year we ask our long-term missionaries and project leaders if there is something a well-qualified small team could do that will enhance and accelerate their work. We make it very clear that they are not to create something for us to do, but that we will come only to serve a real ministry need. Our desire is to assist them in something they feel is necessary and helpful. Our promise is that we will send them the best possible team to serve them in the accomplishment of that task. We do not want to lead and we do not want to take charge, but we do want to serve. The number of teams we send out is contingent on the number of places where our service would be useful.

In his encouragement of this strategy, David Platt says, "Short-term missions done right helps fuel long-term disciple-making on a field. So that happens really through deep partnership with those who are serving alongside another context. So to have deep partnership with churches and ministry partners and mission partners who are doing long-term disciple-making and have identified ways where a short-term team can help fuel a long-term disciple-making process can be hugely helpful for the spread of the gospel on the field."[65] To help us have a greater effect, it is our desire to build relationships where we can continually send teams and participate

---

[65] Piper and Mathis 2012, 159.

in the progress of the ministry over the long haul. The caution here is to do it in such a way that does not create a crippling dependency. To help alleviate the dependency we will come alongside the local ministry to offer support but will not provide the leadership or be the sole provider of the resources.

Qualified Participants

This is the "who" of short-term ministry. Acts 13 makes it clear that the church in Antioch sent out their best when they sent Barnabas and Saul on that first missionary journey. We want to demonstrate the same commitment for those we send as our long-term missionaries as well as our short-term team members. This will of necessity narrow the field of who serves, but mission trips are not about us, but about the progress of the gospel. I do not prescribe to the view that every believer ought to go on a mission trip or that we ought to send out as many as we can so they can be exposed to missions. I do believe in effective service and maximizing the gifts of God's people, but short-term missions cannot just be about exposure. Exposure is a by-product of sending our very best with an attitude to serve.

We have established a number of criteria to help us objectively measure whom we should send. The applicant for a short-term team

- must be a member of the church, indicating their commitment to its life, ministry, and leadership;
- must be a participant in a church small group where they are learning, loving, and being held accountable in the context of community;
- must be active in a church ministry where they are demonstrating their gifts and skills in ministry;
- must have the gifts, skills, and experience necessary to participate in the project; and

- must have successfully completed the short-term missions training course in which they are introduced to the basics of cross-cultural ministry.

Why do we set these standards? Because short-term missions is not just a trip. It is not a vacation or fancy shopping excursion. It is the extension of the ministry already taking place in the life of the team member. Short-term ministry is an extension of who they are and what they are already doing in ministry. Although their overseas ministry experience will sharpen their thinking and help polish their gifts, it is not designed as a place for the untested servant to figure out who they are. If they have not served at home, what makes us think they will suddenly be converted into a great servant once they are overseas?

I learned this lesson the hard way while helping lead a short-term team. On a particular evening we had invited all the young boys and teens to gather on the local soccer field for a game. Because they were Europeans and we were Canadians, we would not have a chance if we played against them. After all, we are not very good at games in which we don't carry a stick. But we took our chances and had a wonderful time. As the game wound down, we planned that to gather the guys around and provide refreshments, giving us an opportunity to share the gospel with them. When I asked one of our team members to share, his answer was an abrupt "No!" His response left me flabbergasted but helped me rethink who it is we should be sending on these teams that are designed to do community outreach.

Adequate Preparation

Besides making some basic decisions about the when, where, and why, and selecting the best-qualified team members, we also ought to make sure we provide each team member with adequate preparation. They have already been tested on the home field, but working cross-culturally is something else. We cannot assume that the activities and thinking of our home will automatically transfer to another part of the world. Time must be given for preparation. Although an entire book could be written about preparing for short-term ministry, here are a few general pointers that need to be considered.

Our preparation must reiterate the importance of going as servants and not as leaders or masters. It is way too easy for our take-charge, get-it-done, do-it-right attitude to be tucked into our suitcase and transported into a culture where it is viewed as unkind, rude, and demeaning. Our task-oriented culture can create huge clashes with the relational-based cultures that describe much of our world.

One of our teams went to Burkina Faso to help with a construction project at the invitation of one of our long-term missionaries. After the team arrived and settled in, they were introduced to the project foreman. He was very nervous about having a group of white men help him. He had never worked with white men before and viewed them as being much superior to him. However, our team reassured him that he would be their boss and that they would do whatever he asked of them. They would haul sand, mix cement, and carry bricks. No task was too menial. The foreman was a bit skeptical at first, but by the end of the two weeks of working together, his farewell comments to the team were, "You have shown me the way of Jesus." The foreman was not a believer, but saw Jesus through the servanthood of the white men, who did not push him out of the way but worked for him.

Our preparation must also push our team members to be students of the country and culture they enter. It is so easy to arrive in another country thinking we know everything about it because we saw a thirty-second snippet about the country on the evening news. I have been embarrassed more than once by well-meaning short-termers who desire to start a conversation with comments like, "I heard that in your country …" and then go on to describe what they heard on a Western news report. The embarrassing part is when the local person says, "It is not that way at all." The lesson: It is far better to ask questions than to make statements. It is far better to learn from the local community than to believe what is seen on the news back home. Our information is quickly spouted but is too often is a display of our ignorance.

In that same vein, we need to help our team members get beyond themselves by being slow to talk about what they have at home or how things are done there. On a trip to an Eastern European country, a team was asked to visit various elementary schools to meet the students and give them some information about Canada. It all sounded really good, until they got to a classroom and came to the end of one of the presentations. The teacher was very unhappy and rebuked the team for their pride in saying their country was better than hers. Rather than simply state the facts, the team had made comparisons to the country they were visiting and had come across as if they were better. We may feel our country is superior and our way of doing things is better, but that is only because we are comfortable with them and for most of us that is all we know. But to communicate that is to perfume the air with superiority that is pride. We do not live in a "better" place because we somehow are better people. We live where we do only by the grace of God, and we cannot and must not appear to take any credit for it or how we do things.

A comprehensive short-term training model ought to cover a number of significant topics:

- A definition of missions
- The church's policies governing short-term missions
- The gospel—What it isn't, what it is, and how to package it for various cultures[66]

---

[66] A great set of resources is Chris Gilbert's *What Is the Gospel?*, Mark Dever's *The Gospel and Personal Evangelism*, and Roland Muller's *Shame and Honor.*

- Spiritual disciplines necessary for ongoing spiritual preparation
- A review of the resources of the short-termer, including spiritual gifts, personality style, language, skills, and education
- How to build a support team for prayer and finances
- Crossing cultural lines and what to expect in different cultures[67]
- Do's and don'ts of interacting with specific cultures and religions
- Practical suggestions for international travel, including health care, vaccinations, appropriate clothing, packing, and crossing borders
- Guidelines for personal and team safety
- How to build a strong team and deal with potential conflict between members
- Coming to terms with home and how to evaluate and continually grow as a result of the short-term experience

Not every problem will be solved or every contingency met through a training program, but it will go a long ways in helping us get beyond ourselves and alleviate some of the damaging clash of cultures. Let me take you back to Burkina Faso for a few moments. One day we were visiting the home of one of the villagers. He invited us to sit by the fire and drink tea with him. While we sat there enjoying his hospitality, he told us that his cow had died because it had eaten one of the prolific black plastic bags that litter the country. The result was that he was unable to plow his field in preparation for planting. As we sat and listened, I could see in the faces of our team members that the solution to the problem was

---

[67] Sarah Lanier's book, *Foreign to Familiar*, serves as a beginning place to help team members understand some of the basic differences between people from hot and cold climates.

not hard to find. The purchase of a new animal was within reach with just the pocket money between us. Having taken a short-term mission basic training course, they knew they were not to pull their wallets out right then and there. That evening during our team meeting, we talked about what we could or should do and decided to talk to the local pastor. Instead of buying a cow, we took a sum of money and gave it to the pastor to establish a benevolent fund that could be wisely administered by the elders of the church to those they felt were in the greatest need.[68] A few days later, we found out that the crisis of the dead cow was not new. The cow had died three years earlier.

How many cows had been paid for by other groups? I never asked. But I do know that taking time to think through the kinds of things to expect in a cross-cultural exchange has saved our teams from buying a lot of unnecessary "cows."

---

[68] "[W]hen local organizations or ministries are willing and able to provide the necessary relief assistance, it is preferable to let them do so. They have the local knowledge about who really needs help and who does not, and they are the ones who will be there conducting ministry long after the STM team has gone. At a minimum, the STM team needs to be seen as an extension of local organizations rather than as independent, outside agents" (Corbett and Fikkert 2009, 156–157).

Summarizing the Principles

1. To be effective, short-term mission trips must be about more than just the benefit to the participants on the team.
2. Churches should develop a set of standards of excellence that will guide the preparation, performance, and follow-up of their short-term teams.
3. A combination of adequate preparation and qualified participants will improve a short-term team's ability to enhance and accelerate the work of overseas partners.

Questions to Consider

1. If you have been involved in a short-term mission trip, why did you go? What did you accomplish? As you look back, was the trip more about you or about serving others?
2. What is the purpose of your church's short-term mission trips? What are the standards that guide this ministry?
3. If you were to improve your church's short-term missions ministry, what would you do? Why?

— Chapter 8 —

By Praying for the Kingdom's Advance

Have you ever stopped to really listen to yourself pray? How much of your praying is about yourself? You know what I mean: your health, your relationships, your finances, your problems, your job, your assignments, your ... your ... your .... Or, how much of the praying you listen to in your small group or with your family is self-centered? I have to confess that too much of my praying is about me and my stuff. It is not wrong to pray about these things, but is that enough? In light of the desperate condition of the lost and the vast needs of the world, how can we get beyond ourselves in our praying?

Listening to Paul Pray

It is amazing what you can learn about a person and their walk with God when you listen to them pray. You find out what they believe about God. You find out what motivates them to press forward in difficult times. You learn about their willingness to rely on God's sovereignty. You learn about the influence and depth of God's Word in their everyday lives. You can learn a lot, just as others who listen to your prayers can learn a lot about you.

Let's listen to the apostle Paul. Certainly there is something we can learn about him and from him in terms of praying for the advance of the kingdom of God. In Romans he thanks God for the believers in that city because their "faith is proclaimed in all the world." He also asks the Lord for an opportunity to visit Rome so that "they might be mutually encouraged by each other's faith" (Romans 1:8–12). For the Corinthians he is thankful for the "grace of God that was given you in Christ Jesus" and the enrichment that is theirs in Christ through the giving of spiritual gifts. He also reminds them of God's sustaining power and faithfulness to carry them "guiltless in the day of our Lord Jesus Christ" (1 Corinthians 1:4–9).

He thanks the Lord for the Ephesians' faith in the Lord and their "love toward all the saints." He asks the Lord to give them "the Spirit of wisdom and of revelation in the knowledge of him" that they may know the hope to which they have been called, the "riches of his glorious inheritance in the saints, what is the immeasurable greatness of his power toward us who believe," and Christ's sovereignty, which is "far above all rule and authority and power and dominion, and above every name that is named, not only in this age but also in the one to come" (Ephesians 1:15–23).

Paul is thankful to the Lord for the Philippians' partnership in the gospel. He prays that their "love may abound more and more, with knowledge and all discernment, so that you may approve what is excellent, and so be pure and blameless for the day of Christ, filled with the fruit of righteousness that comes through Jesus Christ, to the glory and praise of God" (Philippians 1:3–11). He is thankful to the Lord for the Colossians' faith and love and prays that they "may be filled with the knowledge of his will in all spiritual wisdom and understanding, so as to walk in a manner worthy of the Lord, fully pleasing to him, bearing fruit in every good work and increasing in the knowledge of God" (Colossians 1:3–14).

In his prayers for the Thessalonians he is thankful for their "work of faith and labor of love and steadfastness of hope in our Lord Jesus Christ" and prays that God will comfort their "hearts and establish them in every good work and word" (1 Thessalonians 1:3; 2:16–17). He also prays "that our God may make you worthy of his calling and may fulfill every resolve for good and every work of faith by his power" (2 Thessalonians 1:11). He thanks God for Timothy and God's call of his life for ministry (2 Timothy 1:3–4). Paul is thankful for Philemon and prays that the sharing of Philemon's faith "may become effective for the full knowledge of every good thing this is in us for the sake of Christ" (Philemon 1:4–6).

Not only are there Paul's prayers, but we also read some of the prayer requests Paul shares with others. In 1 Timothy 2:1–6 he urges that "supplications, prayers, intercessions, and thanksgivings be made for all people, for kings and all who are in high positions, that we may lead a peaceful and quiet life, godly and dignified in every way. This is good, and it is pleasing in the sight of God our Savior, who desires all people to be saved and to come to the knowledge of the truth. For there is one God, and there is one mediator between God and men, the man Christ Jesus, who gave himself as a ransom for all, which is the testimony given at the proper time."

He requests prayer from the Colossians "that God may open to us a door for the word, to declare the mystery of Christ, on account of which I am in prison." He goes on and asks them to pray that he might be able to clearly communicate the message as he ought (Colossians 4:3–4). From the Thessalonians he requests prayer "that the word of the Lord may speed ahead and be honored, as happened among you, and that we may be delivered from wicked and evil men. For not all have faith." As he requests prayer, he encourages them with the promise that "the Lord is faithful. He will establish you and guard you against the evil one" (2 Thessalonians 3:1–3). As he writes from his prison cell in Rome, he invites the Ephesian church to be "praying at all times in the Spirit, with all prayer and supplication. To that end keep alert with all perseverance, making supplication for all the saints, and also for me, that words may be given to me in opening my mouth boldly to proclaim the mystery of the gospel, for which I am an ambassador in chains, that I may declare it boldly, as I ought to speak" (Ephesians 6:18–20).

Each of these passages is loaded with nuggets of wonderful

truth that we could mine and linger over for some time. But did you catch the flavor of prayer as it is reflected in these verses? Paul's prayers are full of thanksgiving for the work of grace in the lives of those who believe. Even in the writing of a difficult letter to the Corinthians he is grateful to God for them and the progress of the gospel in their lives. He prays over and over again for the deepening of faith and growth in the knowledge of the Lord and his love and power. He prays that they will be wise and live lives that reflect the wonder of Christ and his gift of forgiveness.

He calls on the early church believers, and us, to get beyond ourselves and to pray for national leaders so that the gospel may go forward and men will be saved. We are to pray for gospel workers that God may open doors and give opportunities to share the gospel in ever widening circles. We are to pray that God's Word will speed ahead and not be hindered by people, politics, or pride. We are to pray that we live lives worthy of the calling and that we might complete the assignments God has given us. We are to pray that the sharing of our faith might be effective.

There is not too much in these verses about praying about our stuff. Rather, they are filled with thanksgiving and requests pertaining to the progress of the gospel in our broken world that desperately needs a Savior.

Learning from the Puritans

Not only do we need to get beyond ourselves in what we pray for, but we also need to get beyond ourselves in how we discipline ourselves to pray. For me, this is the tough part about praying. It is not hard to affirm the need for prayer, agree that we need to realign our prayers with the purposes of God, enjoy amazing stories of answers to prayer, and say "Amen" to the prayers of others. But what about actually praying? That is the hard part. It is hard to discipline ourselves and move away from our natural tendency toward halfhearted praying and prayerlessness.

The Puritans of the sixteenth, seventeenth, and early eighteenth centuries were known for prayer. Among them were men such as Richard Baxter (*The Reformed Pastor*), John Bunyan (*Pilgrim's Progress*), Isaac Watts (hymn writer), John Foxe (*Book of Martyrs*), and Jonathan Edwards (early eighteenth century). In his book *Living for God's Glory*, Joel Beeke tells us it is from their prayer lives that we learn a number of things we can use to keep us from lapsing into half-hearted prayer.[69]

First, we need to give priority to prayer. We need to understand that prayer is the first and most important thing we are called to do. John Bunyan of the 1600's is quoted as saying, "You can do more than pray after you have prayed, but you cannot do more than pray until you have prayed", and "Pray often, for prayer is a shield to the soul, a sacrifice to God, and a scourge to Satan."

Second, we need to give ourselves to prayer. This means more than just some of our time or adding it to our daily list of activities to complete. It means prayer must become the very essence of our spiritual life and work. Prayer measures the health of our soul.

Third, we need to give room to prayer. We need to find or create a specific, private place for prayer. We need to block out definite times for prayer in our daily routine. Between those definite times, we need to commit ourselves to pray in response to the slightest impulse to do so.

Fourth, give the Word to prayer. Pray with Scripture, reminding God of his own words, pleading with him to do as he has promised. Pray that he would keep his promises and reveal his glory and power and love. He has spoken and will do as he has said. As well, pray through the Scriptures. As you read and reflect on a passage of Scripture, invite God to deepen the truths of that passage in your own life. Invite him to specifically change the way you think, the way you talk, the way you act and react in light of the specific timeless principles found in the passage. Ask him to

---

[69] Beeke, 2008, 207.

powerfully apply the truth to your life and situations and ministry assignments.

Fifth and finally, give God-centeredness to prayer. Prayer is not about us. It is about God. He is the center of the universe, we are not. Prayer is God's gift to us and involves interaction with and among the Father, Son, and the Holy Spirit. It's not merely an exercise where we ask God to move on our behalf. It is a privilege whereby we have the invitation and opportunity to interact with God in the unfolding of his meticulously sovereign plan for the universe and the ages.

Lord, Bless the Missionaries

"Lord, bless the missionaries, wherever they are and whatever they are doing today. Amen." That's the kind of missionary prayers many of us have grown up with. It seems like a great prayer that covers all the bases. It is addressed to the Lord. It asks for blessings and assumes the Lord knows what ought to fit in that category. It covers all geographical contingencies. Besides, it is not like the Lord has lost track of one or two of his servants and needs to be reminded of where they are. It also takes care of all the activities a missionary might be participating in on any given day. The prayer also closes with the obligatory "Amen" we have been taught is needed to make it an official prayer. Since the prayer is short, we are not taking a lot of the Lord's time; we are praying for our missionaries, but we are not taking time away from the "to do" list and the responsibilities that govern our lives each day. I think we've got it covered with what seems like a win-win-win prayer.

Or is it? How do we know what *bless* means or when God has blessed? How do we know the missionaries are where they ought to be and doing what they ought to be doing? Do we know what our missionaries think about this kind of praying? Are they confident that our prayers are adequate for the pressures and concerns of their day? How do we know such prayers have not just become trite religious words that have little meaning and no effect on the real world?

Praying the Specifics

What are the specifics of praying for kingdom advance? How can we become unambiguous in our prayers? How can we apply the lessons from Paul's prayers and the thinking of the Puritans and turn them into a rigorous but invigorating prayer life? How can we get beyond ourselves and develop a global perspective in our praying? Here are some suggestions.

First, pray through world events. We live in a time in history when it seems the world is convulsing. We barely get through one global crisis when another comes crashing onto the scene like ocean waves on a beach. The political, financial, religious, medical, ideological, environmental and meteorological breakers are heaped up to become one great tsunami of devastation. The world is filled with bad news that is terrifying and discouraging.

As believers in Christ, we must anchor ourselves in the comprehensive sovereignty of God. He calls us to "Remember this and stand firm ... for I am God, and there is no other; I am God, and there is none like me, declaring the end from the beginning and from ancient times things not yet done, saying, 'My counsel shall stand, and I will accomplish all my purpose' ... I have spoken, and I will bring it to pass; I have purposed and I will do it" (Isaiah 46:8–11). We can be assured that all the events of the time in which we are living are under the sovereign hand of God and he is directing all things toward his predetermined ends. His eternal purposes shall stand and he is not taken by surprise, nor will he be thwarted by the events of the world. Rather, in his sovereignty, he is moving all the events and people of the world toward the accomplishment of his purposes. The stories of history are not the stories of man alone, but are the stories of God, who planned the whole course of history to result in his glorification. As a result we can pray with confidence and joy, knowing that all the bad news we hear and feel is under the control of our Lord.

With this in cemented in our hearts and minds, we can prayerfully wade into the ocean of daily bad news and pray that God will be glorified and that his will done on earth as it is in heaven. We can pray that through these events his kingdom will come. We can pray that individuals who are caught up in the tragedies of sin will see their need for an eternal Savior and will have opportunity to hear the glorious message of his grace. We can pray that the shaking of the nations will result in the growth of the church. We can pray that people will not "refuse him who is speaking. For if they did not escape when they refused him who warned them on earth, much less will we escape if we reject him who warns from heaven" (Hebrews 12:25). Instead of living in fear, "let us be grateful for receiving a kingdom that cannot be shaken, and thus let us offer to God acceptable worship, with reverence and awe, for our God is a consuming fire" (Hebrews 12:28–29).

Second, pray for specific nations and their leaders. Each year Open Doors publishes a World Watch List[70] consisting of the top fifty countries of the world in terms of the persecution of Christians of all denominations. The focus is on persecution for their faith, not persecution for political, economic, social, ethnic, or accidental reasons. This list makes a great place to start praying for specific nations. Pray "for kings and all who are in high positions" (1 Timothy 2:2). Pray that decisions would be made that would result in the progress of the gospel in their nation. Pray for believers that words may be given to them and that they would be bold and clear in the proclamation of the gospel message even though they may face persecution (Ephesians 6:19–20).

Third, pray for specific missionaries. Adopt a few and commit yourself to praying for them regularly—not the "bless the missionaries" kind of praying, but praying around specific needs and

---

[70] At time of writing this list could be found at www.worldwatchlist.us.

situations. Become a giant in prayer on their behalf. For this, you will need to maintain contact with them. One missionary writes, "Missionaries don't escape trials, misfortune or injustice. They may lose children, be stricken with cancer, and the list goes on. I am inclined to believe that missionaries are one of the enemy's favorite targets because front-line ministry puts us in the crosshairs of evil minions. The kingdom of darkness hates the kingdom of light. The Apostle Paul must have known this because he reminded people of his ongoing need for others to pray for him. Imagine that: the spiritual leader, Paul, needed prayer giants in his life."[71]

Pray for their travel, not just the air travel to and from the country, but the daily travel they must do in the country. Some of the most dangerous travel situations that I have faced have been on the roads of other countries. More than once I have concluded that I was headed straight to the gates of heaven while a passenger in someone else's vehicle. As one of my ministry friends said, "There are four parts of safe road travel: good roads, good cars, good drivers, and the grace of God." Then he went on to say that in his country, they have only one out of the four: the grace of God.

Pray for their physical health. They are exposed to all sorts of things that we take for granted. On a visit to Delhi, my wife marveled at how dark the white facecloth became when washing her face at the end of a day. The air is so dirty in many of the world's cities that it sticks to your skin. Pray for issues related to safe food and water. We might benefit from programs and policies designed to keep our food safe, but these kinds of regulations are often unheard of in other countries.

Pray for personal spiritual nurture and growth. Many of our missionaries, especially among unreached people, do not have the benefit of a church to attend. They do not have a pastor who speaks regularly into their lives through the preaching of the Word. They do not have access to all the spiritually nurturing resources

[71] Stott, 2005.

we often take for granted here at home. They often are the ones who give and give and give, and unless they can find some way to be spiritually refueled, they will run empty. It is then that they are most easily discouraged, get embroiled in conflict, become defeated, and are open to temptation.

Pray for the missionary's family. If they are married, pray that their marriage will reflect the love of Christ for his bride and the submission of Christ to his Father. Pray for their children, that they would grow to be those who also love and live for the Lord. Pray that the father would not forget the responsibility to first disciple his own children. Pray that the children will not resent God's call on their parents and turn away from the Lord. Pray for purity, particularly for those who are single and may be feeling lonely.

Pray for their ongoing ministry focus. Pray that they will not forget the reason they are where they are. Pray that the heart of the mission, the message of God's grace, will be central to all they do. Pray that they will have open doors and opportunities to declare the message of grace. Pray they will not be distracted by the good at the expense of the best. Pray that they will not be fearful, but remain faithful and that those who are the Lord's in their place of ministry will hear and respond to God's call to salvation (Acts 18:10).

Pray for their financial needs. Pray that they will have enough to do what God has called them to do. Pray that they will not be distracted by their financial situation and lose focus. Pray that the Lord will raise up faithful supporters who are willing to live simply so that they can give generously to the cause of the gospel. Pray that the Lord will challenge you in this area of stewardship.

Pray for team relationships. The greatest points of stress for a missionary are not the weather, their finances or lack thereof, the political tensions of the country, or their workload. One of the greatest problems that missionaries have on the field is other missionaries. I have heard this over and over again. And since our enemy is a great liar, he loves to stir up conflict by getting us to believe lies about each other. Satan will do all he can to get a team to criticize, mistrust, undermine, and tear each other apart. Pray that each member of the missionary team will put away falsehood, speak the truth with his neighbor, be angry yet not sin or let the sun go down on his anger, and give no opportunity to the devil (Ephesians 4:25–27). Pray that "all bitterness and wrath and anger and clamor and slander be put away" from them, "along with all malice." Pray that they will "be kind to one another, tenderhearted, forgiving one another, as God in Christ forgave" them (Ephesians 4:31–32).

Pray for their safety. Paul called on the Thessalonians to "Pray for us, that the word of the Lord may speed ahead and be honored, as happened among you, and that we may be delivered from wicked and evil men. For not all have faith" (2 Thessalonians 3:1–2). Safety is an important thing to pray for, but beyond that, pray for their trust in God. As one person said, uncertainty soon shows "who is trusting their passport rather than their God to protect them."[72]

Just in case you thought we were almost finished with praying, let me add a couple more items to your prayer list. The fourth main prayer request is for more workers. This prayer was commanded by Jesus in the book of Matthew.

> And Jesus went throughout all the cities and villages, teaching in their synagogues and proclaiming the gospel of the kingdom and healing every disease and every affliction. When he saw the crowds, he had compassion for them, because they were harassed and helpless, like sheep without a shepherd. Then he said to his disciples, "The harvest is plentiful, but the laborers are few; therefore pray earnestly to the Lord at the harvest to send out laborers into his harvest." (Matthew 9:35–38)

---

[72] Corwin, 2009.

The fifth prayer focus for missions is probably the greatest. Pray that God would be glorified in all things. John Piper brings this into focus when he writes:

> The first two petitions of the Lord's prayer are perhaps the clearest statement in the teachings of Jesus that missions is driven by the passion of God to be glorified among the nations. "Hallowed by your name. Your kingdom come" (Matt. 6:9–10). Here Jesus teaches us to ask God to hallow his name and to make his kingdom come. This is a missionary prayer. Its aim is to engage the passions of God for his name among those who forget or revile the name of God (Pss. 9:17; 74:18). To hallow God's name means to put it in a class by itself and to cherish and honor it above every claim to our allegiance or affection. Jesus' primary concern— the very first petition of the prayer he teaches—is that more and more people, and more and more peoples, come to hallow God's name. This is the reason the universe exists. Missions exists because this hallowing does not.[73]

With this much to pray about, we must get beyond ourselves and develop the discipline needed to actually pray. We have been invited to lay our own needs before the throne of grace, but let's not quickly dash away in pursuit of our dreams and plans. Let's develop a grander view of the magnificent work of God in our messy world and willingly and joyfully participate in it on our knees.

---

[73] Piper, 2010, 58.

Summarizing the Principles

1. You can learn a great deal about a person and their walk with God when you listen to their prayers.
2. An examination of the prayers of Paul reveals that the progress of the gospel was central to his praying.
3. From the Puritans we learn that prayer is a priority discipline to which we give ourselves. It is a privilege whereby we have the invitation and opportunity to interact with God in the unfolding of his meticulously sovereign plan for the universe and the ages.
4. Our praying must expand beyond "God bless the missionaries" to include specific requests focused on the life and context of specific missionaries.

Questions to Consider

1. What would people learn about you and your trust in God if they listened carefully to your prayers?
2. Reflect on the typical prayer gathering at your church. What is central to the prayer requests that are shared? How often do the requests focus on what is central to the heart of God?
3. When you pray for missionaries, what do you pray for? How might you become more specific in your praying? What could you add to your prayer list?

— Chapter 9 —

By Finishing Well

Among the things I enjoy in life, two stand out. One is my motor-cycle and the other is my hammock. The motorcycle represents my urge to go and do and explore and conquer the world around me. At the twist of the throttle there is risk, exhilaration, and the delight of experiencing the raw world. On a motorcycle my sensitivity to the weather, the road conditions, the flow of traffic, and the environment are all heightened. There is the rush of the wind, the smell of the land, and the unobstructed view along with the rumble of the engine. The motorcycle provides an experience that continually fluctuates between peaceful contentment on quiet, straight roads and adrenaline-charged excitement that comes with tight corners or erratic traffic. Then there is my hammock. Strung between two posts in my backyard, it is the place I love to go and rest at the end of a long day. It takes only seconds for me to fall asleep in the warmth of the evening sunshine. It represents my desire to rest and relax and take it easy.

As I get older and more reflective, I think the motorcycle is characteristic of my earlier years of drive and ambition when I wanted to conquer the world. It represents my desire to go and do and accomplish and master. But as time passes, I find the hammock to be a growing influence in my life. As it gently swings in the breeze, I become less and less influenced by or concerned about the rush of the world around me, and more and more absorbed in myself.

Don't get me wrong. There is nothing wrong with resting. We all need it regularly. But I wonder if my growing love for the hammock is characteristic of something that so readily happens in life. As time progresses, we lose our edge, we are no longer are driven by passion, and we are less likely to pour out our lives in serving others. We would rather lie in the hammock and have someone serve us lemonade that is not too sour and not too sweet. After all we have done, we deserve it!

Get Out of the Hammock

But as I open my Bible, I am shocked back into reality with the words of Paul. As he faces his impending death, he writes of himself, "For I am already being poured out as a drink offering, and the time of my departure has come. I have fought the good fight. I have finished the race, I have kept the faith. Henceforth there is laid up for me the crown of righteousness, which the Lord, the righteous Jude, will award to me on that Day, and not only to me but also to all who have loved his appearing" (2 Timothy 4:6–8). For him there was no hammock in the latter part of life. There was no resignation, but a fight to be continued and a race to be finished. In describing his appearance before the court of Rome, he says, "At my first defense no one came to stand by me, but all deserted me. May it not be charged against them! But the Lord stood by me and strengthened me." Paul then goes on to tell why the Lord strengthened him: "so that through me the message might be fully proclaimed and all the Gentiles might hear it" (4:16–17). At the very heart of all Paul did and experienced was the passion to have the gospel fully proclaimed. Even in the last days of his life, there was no hammock, but a push to reach the unreached. He was pushed to finish well and complete the lifelong assignment given him by God. As he stretched out toward the finish line, he put all he had into it because he knew "The Lord will rescue me from every evil deed and bring me safely into his heavenly kingdom. To him be the glory forever and ever. Amen" (4:18).

To finish well, we must get beyond ourselves. We must climb out of our hammocks and get back in the fight, get back in the race. We must get beyond thinking we have already done our part. We must get beyond thinking we are deserving of rest. We must get beyond ourselves and our right to have a physical retirement that too often slips into a spiritual retirement. We need to live radically sold out to finishing the task of reaching the unreached.

The Bible gives us a great reason for pressing on. It is found in Matthew 24. In that chapter Jesus describes for his disciples what the world will be like as it rushes toward the brink of time. He describes terrible calamities that parallel the bad news we hear on a daily basis, including war and rumors of war, and earthquakes and famines in various places. In his description of the signs of his coming, he describes hatred toward the church by all nations and the persecution of believers. He foretells the coming of false prophets who will lead many astray. With the increased unruliness spreading through the world, he tells us, the love of many will grow cold. At the conclusion of this picture he says two very important things that become reasons for finishing well. First, he tells us that "the one who endures to the end will be saved (24:13). Second, he says, "And this gospel of the kingdom will be proclaimed throughout the whole world as a testimony to all nations, and then the end will come" (24:14).

Our pressing on will not save us but will be evidence that we are saved. The Bible clearly teaches that those who are genuinely saved from the wrath of God through faith in Christ will continue in the Christian life until death and then go to be with Christ in heaven.[74] The Bible also teaches that those who persevere to

---

[74] John 3:36; 5:24; 6:4–7; 6:38–40; 10:27–29; Romans 8:1; Romans 8:30; Ephesians 1:13–14; 1 Peter 1:5; 1 John 5:13.

the end have been truly redeemed[75] and that those who fall away may give many external indications of being saved without really experiencing redemption.[76] Finishing well and persevering in the faith and pushing further toward godliness is evidence of genuine conversion. Those who are truly saved will press on and endure to the end.

We have reason to press on not only in our personal faith, but in our ministry. Jesus indicates that it is only after the gospel of the kingdom is proclaimed to all nations or ethnic groups that will the end come. Jesus knows those that are his, having chosen them before the foundation of the world, and only when they have all come to faith will the end come and the Lord return. Peter reemphasizes this when he responds to the question of his day: "Where is the promise of his coming" (2 Peter 3:4). As we review history from our perspective, it has already been almost a 2000-year wait since the promise of his return. What is taking so long? Peter responds with "The Lord is not slow to fulfill his promise as some count slowness, but is patient toward you, not wishing that any should perish, but that all should reach repentance" (3:9). The Lord is patiently waiting until all those chosen before the foundation of the world hear his call and respond in repentance and faith. When the job of missions is finished, the Lord will return! And until the Lord returns, the job of missions is not finished. Our response: let's get beyond ourselves and climb out of the hammock and press on!

The Convictions of Our Minds

The place to begin in our press forward is in our minds. There are some essential convictions we must grab on to that will steer us toward the finish line. These are the things that need to firmly planted in our minds and guide us as we make decisions about our

---

[75] 1 Peter 1:5; John 8:31–32; Matthew 10:22; Colossians 1:22–23; Hebrews 3:14.
[76] Matthew 7:21–23; Mark 4:16–17; Galatians 6:2; 2 Corinthians 11:15, 26.

investments. The following principles have been adapted from the list of essential convictions developed by Paul Washer and Heart Cry Missionary Society.[77] The first is that mission work is an impossibility apart from the power of God. We are not on a man-made adventure where we get to do all the planning, preparation, and implementation. This is a God-sized mission that takes his power to accomplish. We need the power of the Holy Spirit to guide us in our recruitment, training, and preparation. We need him to move in the hearts of people so that we will have the resources we need to accomplish our assignment. We need him to convict and draw to Christ those with whom we share the gospel. We need his power to keep faithful those who respond to the gospel. We need him to open God's Word and illuminate the hearts and minds of those we teach and push toward leadership. This is God's mission, and as Jesus said, "Without me you can do nothing."

Second, the true gospel must be proclaimed. It is the proclamation of the gospel that changes lives, not our strategies or our programs. I shuddered when I recently heard a television preacher declare that his program changes lives. Paul declared the gospel "is the power of God for salvation to everyone who believes (Romans 1:16). Therefore we ought to focus our efforts on the proclamation of that gospel and make sure we are proclaiming a biblical gospel and not just our comfortable, culturally acceptable version with its warm fuzziness and cuddly Jesus.

The third conviction we need to plant in our minds is that the gospel transcends culture. No matter where they live or what they believe, it is the gospel that men and women need to hear. Although the cultural context and differences need to be considered, it is more important for the missionary to be biblically sensitive than culturally sensitive. People are saved from the wrath of God only

---

[77] The list of Essential Convictions and their explanations can be found in detail at the website of Heart Cry Missionary Society (www.heartcrymissionary.com/about-us/statement-of-faith/essential-convictions).

through the proclamation of the gospel. People will continue to grow in their faith only through the careful teaching of the whole counsel of the Word of God. Missionary work needs to be centered on and saturated with God's Word.

Fourth, incarnational missions are essential. Although there are many ways to communicate the gospel, including films, TV, the Internet, and various forms of social media, there is no substitute for a believer purposefully living among a group of people to declare, teach, and live out the gospel. It is over the longer course of time that the gospel is seen to be real and relevant.

The fifth conviction is in keeping with the fourth, and is a hard one for many to accept: superficial evangelism is one of the greatest hindrances to effective missions. "Non-theological preaching, entertaining skits, and gospel films are no substitute for the biblical exposition of the gospel. Inviting men to raise their hands and pray a prayer is no substitute for the biblical call to repentance, faith, and personal discipleship. Biblical assurance of salvation does not flow from a past decision or a prayer, but from the examination of one's enduring lifestyle in the light of Scripture."[78]

Conviction number six: Church planting is the primary work of missions. The biblical record is clear in that everywhere the early missionary team went, they proclaimed the gospel with the intent of planting a church. In each city they preached the gospel and gathered together those who had come to faith in communities called the church. The long-term influence of the gospel on a community does not take place when an evangelist comes to town and holds a series of meetings. The long-term influence comes when a local church is established and continues to reach out to its community and beyond, generation after generation.

Seventh, missions is costly. "Amy Carmichael explained that missions is no more and no less than an opportunity to die. We live in a fallen world that is at enmity with God and opposes His truth;

---

[78] Washer, 2010.

therefore, missions and suffering go hand in hand. Any advancement of the kingdom of Christ into the dominion of the devil will be met with warfare. There are many countries and people groups where martyrdom cannot be avoided."[79]

To this list of seven, let me add an eighth: Missions is the greatest assignment and investment we could ever make in life. Why? Missions is about eternity. Missions is about participating in the great purposes of God that will far outlast the entire span of human history. If you want to leave a legacy, there will be none greater than that which propels the gospel forward and participates in the completion of the glorification of God through the redemption of those he has chosen to be his redeemed children. This is not only the greatest purpose, but the main purpose of every believer. When Jesus called the disciples to follow him, he told them that becoming "fishers of men" would be the result. It would be the natural outcome of following him. Missions is not something we must add to the agenda of our lives. Reaching the unreached and making disciples of all nations becomes the purpose of our lives and the natural outflow of our worship of Christ.

The Discipline of Our Hearts

Although the head stuff is great, it is not enough. To get beyond ourselves and finish well, we need to make a commitment of our hearts that pushes what we believe into a passionate response. The first step is to get beyond our spiritual arrogance and gospel self-centeredness. It seems like the longer we are saved, the more we tend to take credit for our lives and the more we believe God got a pretty good deal when he got us. But just when I begin to think like that, the Holy Spirit drags me back to the Word, where I read of the lostness of my soul and the repugnance of my sin. Paul's familiar sermons in 1 Corinthians 6 and Ephesians 2 shout at me:

---

[79] Ibid.

" ... do you not know that the unrighteous will not inherit the kingdom of God? Do not be deceived: neither the sexually immoral, nor idolaters, nor adulterers, nor men who practice homosexuality, nor thieves, nor the greedy, nor drunkards, nor revilers, nor swindlers will inherit the kingdom of God. And such were some of you" (1 Corinthians 6:9–11). "And you were dead in the trespasses and sins in which you once walked, following the course of this world, following the prince of the power of the air, the spirit that is now at work in the sons of disobedience—among whom we all once lived in the passions of our flesh, carrying out the desires of the body and the mind, and were by nature children of wrath, like the rest of mankind" (Ephesians 2:1–3).

A child of wrath! I am one whose life will someday be wrapped up and presented to God, and all my smugness will be wiped away with the words of condemnation that I have duly earned for my sin and rebellion against him. This is who I was and who I am apart from Christ. This is the sum total of everyone who has lived, is living, and will ever live.

But as I cringe under the burden of these thoughts, I hear the rest of Paul's sermons and am washed over with joy at God's mercy and grace:

> But God, being rich in mercy, because of the great love with which he loved us, even when we were dead in our trespasses, made us alive together with Christ—by grace you have been saved—and raised us up with him and seated us with him in the heavenly places in Christ Jesus, so that in the coming ages he might show the immeasurable riches of his grace in kindness toward us in Christ Jesus. For by grace you have been saved through faith. And this is not your own doing; it is the gift of God, not a result of works, so that no one may boast. (Ephesians 2:4–9)

"And you, who were dead in your trespasses and the uncircumcision of your flesh, God made alive together with him, having forgiven us all our trespasses, by canceling the record of debt that stood against us with its legal demands. This he set aside, nailing it to the cross" (Colossians 2:13–14). "But you were washed, you were sanctified, you were justified in the name of the Lord Jesus Christ and by the Spirit of our God" (1 Corinthians 6:11). "There is therefore now no condemnation for those who are in Christ Jesus" (Romans 8:1).

I who was once an object of God's wrath have become, by his grace, an object of his mercy. I who once deserved eternal condemnation have become a recipient of his eternal blessing. But it was not I; it was him who made it all possible. I must never grow arrogant, but always remember where I came from. I was who once in need of missions.

Not only must I get beyond my arrogance, but I must get beyond the laziness and lack of discipline that keeps me from building my life on God's Word. For too many of us our approach to the Bible is "been there, done that." We have been around the church so long, heard so many sermons, and attended so many Bible studies and classes that it is all old stuff to us. Our faith is no longer vibrant and growing, but is simply something we hang on to just in case we need it. David Bryant writes about this complacency:

In so many of our churches, I fear, Jesus is regularly deployed as our mascot, as if our life struggles were something like a football game. Once a week on Sunday, Jesus is presented as if He were something like a mascot, trotted out to the field to cheer us up, to give us new vigor and vision, to reassure us that we are "somebodies." We invite Him to reinforce us for the great things we want to do for God. He rebuilds our confidence. He gives us reasons to cheer. He confirms for us over and over that all must be well. We're so proud of Him! We're so happy to be identified with His name. Enthusiasm for Him energizes us—for a while.

But then, for the rest of the week, He is pretty much relegated to the sidelines. For all practical purposes, we are the ones who call the shots. We implement the plays, scramble for first downs and improvise in a pinch. Even if we do it in His name, we do it with little reliance on His person. There's scant evidence that we think of ourselves as somehow utterly incapable of doing anything of eternal consequence apart from Him.

As contradictory as it may seem, many of us have redefined Jesus into someone we can both admire and ignore at the same time! To be our mascot, we've redesigned Him to be reasonably convenient—someone praiseworthy, to be sure, but overall kept in reserve, useful, "on call" as required. We've come to Him as far as we need Him, and no further.

If we insist on Jesus coming along with us as a helper in our games and excellent adventures, we will inevitably tame Him as our mascot.[80]

In response to the sloppy Christian living we so easily fall into, James calls on us to live a disciplined life. Because "God opposes the proud, but gives grace to the humble," he says, "Submit yourselves therefore to God. Resist the devil, and he will flee from you. Draw near to God, and he will draw near to you. Cleanse your hands, you sinners, and purify your hearts, you double-minded. Be wretched and mourn and weep. Let your laughter be turned to mourning and your joy to gloom. Humble yourselves before the Lord, and

---

[80] Bryant, 2009, 720.

he will exalt you" (James 4:6–10). Submitting, resisting, drawing near, confessing, mourning, and humbling are hard things. Because they are not naturally our bent, we need to develop discipline and accountability that will push us to daily be in the Word, regularly deal with our sin, and keep us in tune with the Lord who has redeemed us.

The Activity of Our Hands and Feet

Finishing well not only includes remembering where we have come from and disciplining ourselves toward growth in godliness, but must translate into the activity of our hands and feet. We need to get beyond collecting more stuff. I understand that renting and owning storage lockers is one of the growing businesses in North America. We have so much stuff that we no longer have room for it in our own homes. We are like the rich man in the New Testament who decided he needed to have bigger barns to store his stuff. But it is all this stuff that distracts us from finishing well. The problem with our chrome idols is that we have to keep polishing them. Maintaining all this stuff gets in the way of focusing on the real purpose of a redeemed life—the declaration of the glory and grace of God.

We need to get beyond our doors. We need to get beyond the doors of our homes and the doors of our churches. All around us are people who are under the wrath of God, and every single day that goes by, they are moving closer and closer to eternal condemnation! They see us drive to church every weekend and they see us come home, but they never hear why. They never hear what we have heard and rejoice in.

We need to get beyond our busy-ness. Our lives are so full of extracurricular activity that we do not have time for prayer, we do not have time for significant personal Bible study, and we do not have time to hang out with the neighbors. We are too busy, and that busy-ness is often connected to the church.

We also need to get beyond our self-pity. Life is filled with stress, anxiety, problems, calamities, and suffering. It is inevitable. But as believers, we need to take comfort in the fact that our difficulties are often what the Lord uses to advance the gospel in the lives of others. Instead of asking, "Why me?" we should be asking, "Who else?" And, "How might the Lord use my experience to present the message of grace to others?" God has told us in 1 Corinthians 1:3–7 that abundant suffering brings a supply of comfort that is more than adequate to meet our needs and meet the needs of others through us. Whatever degree of suffering I have endured will equip me to serve others who likewise endure affliction. So instead of wallowing in self-pity, let's finish well by allowing our difficulties to point others to the grace of our Lord Jesus.

We also need to get beyond our retirement. John Piper puts it so much better than I could:

> Two phenomena in America are emerging together: One is the challenge to give our all to do our part in finishing the task of world missions, and the other is a huge baby-boom bulge in the population reaching peak earning years and heading toward "retirement." How will the Christians in this group respond to the typical American dream? Is it a biblical dream? Ralph Winter asks, "Where in the Bible do they see [retirement]? Did Moses retire? Did Paul retire? Peter? John? Do military officers retire in the middle of war?" I mentioned earlier that Oswald Sanders ministered around the world until he died at ninety and that he wrote a book a year between the ages of seventy and eighty-nine.[81]

Piper urges us to see retirement as a new opportunity to impact the unreached peoples of the earth.

---

[81] Piper, 2010, 126–127.

I am saying a new chapter of life opens for most people at age sixty-five. And if we have armed ourselves with the "thought" of the suffering Savior and saturated our mind with the way of the supremacy of God, we will invest our time and energy in this final chapter very differently than if we take our cues from the American dream. Millions of "retired" people should be engaged at all levels of intensity in hundreds of assignments around the world. Talk about travel! Park the RVs and use the senior discounts and "super savers" to fly wherever the agencies have need. Let the unreached peoples of the earth reap the benefits of a lifetime of earning. "You will be repaid at the resurrection of the just" (Luke 14:14).[82]

Finally, let's get beyond our shortsightedness. There is coming a day when we will stand before our glorious Lord and King and will worship in his awesome blazing presence. In that moment and the eternal moments to follow we will not regret the sacrifice, the hardship, the pain, or the suffering that we might have endured in reaching the unreached with the glorious message of grace. "Therefore, my beloved brothers, be steadfast, immovable, always abounding in the work of the Lord, knowing that in the Lord your labor is not in vain" (1 Corinthians 15: 58).

Give Everything You Can

There is a story told by Michael Ramsden in *Finish the Mission* that is worth retelling. It is the story of a man named John Bechtel, who grew up as the son of a missionary family in China. When things became difficult, he was shipped off to school in Hong Kong, and his parents were later expelled from China along with all the other missionaries in about 1949. Years later the Lord laid it on his heart to start an orphanage in Hong Kong. On arriving back in Hong Kong, he realized that he and the governor had been in the same class for seven years. So he went to visit him, and after sharing old school

---

[82] Ibid., 129.

stories over dinner, John told the governor what he wanted to do and asked for land on which to build the orphanage. The answer was no. In fact, everywhere he went and with everyone he talked, the answer always came back the same.

One day he was walking through a particular part of Hong Kong where he discovered a school that was closed. There was a For Sale sign outside, and he knew it would be the perfect place for an orphanage. Once again he contacted everyone he knew in the city, but he couldn't raise the money. No one was interested. An American friend came to visit him, heard about his dream, and invited him back to the States to do a preaching tour where he could tell the story and try to raise the funds. So away he went. When John returned to Hong Kong a month later, he received a brown envelope. Inside was a letter from his American friend along with another envelope. His friend wrote, "John, out of all the churches you preached in and from everyone you met, we have received only one gift." That gift was in the other envelope. When he opened the second envelope he found a letter from a twelve-year-old girl, who had been saving up her allowance and finally had one dollar. In the envelope were the dollar and a note that said, "I would like to give one dollar for the purchase of this orphanage."

John was heartbroken. But as he prayed about it, he decided to go and talk to the caretaker of the empty school building. When he rang the bell, the caretaker came to the iron gates. John said, "I would like you to pass this offer to the owners of this building for me to purchase it." He handed the caretaker the note from the girl with the one-dollar bill in it. The caretaker laughed and tossed it aside. But John let it be known in no uncertain terms that if the caretaker refused to pass on this legitimate offer to the owners of the building, John would take him to court for breach of contract law and in violation of the regulations concerning the sale of buildings in Hong Kong. Shaken, the caretaker picked up the letter and promised to pass it on to the owners. One week later John was contacted by the owners of the building. They told him,

"We have read that little girl's letter. And we are so touched we will agree to sell this building to you for one dollar."[83]

You may feel you don't have much to offer the Lord, but when you offer it all, He can and will do astounding things. Be courageous! The great commission ends with this promise: "I am with you always, to the end of the age" (Matthew 28:20). Whatever God has called you to do, finish it well.

I was recently on a flight from my home to Europe. After we boarded and got settled, all the usual things that take place in the departure of an aircraft unfolded according to plan. The doors were closed, the passengers were instructed on safety procedures, and the ground crew finished stowing the baggage and locking the cargo doors. All seemed to go according to plan. The special truck that pushes the plane away from the jetway was attached and began to move the aircraft toward the location where it could proceed on its own power. On completing its task, the truck was disconnected, and it proceeded to repeat the procedure for the next departing flight. All seemed well. But it wasn't. The truck driver had not finished well, and the aircraft was not in the correct place and couldn't proceed toward the taxiway and runway. As a result, we waited an additional thirty or forty minutes for another truck to rescue us and move us to the appropriate starting point. Sounds like no big deal. The difference in the distance to be pushed by the truck was only a couple of hundred meters or so. But as a result of one man not finishing his task well, no matter how insignificant it might have seemed, hundreds of people on the other side of the world, plus those of us on the plane, were affected when connecting flights were missed.

You may feel like that insignificant truck driver. But the assignment God has given you in his kingdom building is vital. Finish well. People all around the world need to hear the message of God's glory and grace. Get beyond yourself and build your life around this grand purpose, and finish well.

---

[83] Piper and Mathis, 2012, 165–166.

Summarizing the Principles

1. To finish well we must get beyond thinking that we have already done our part and are deserving of rest.
2. To finish well we need to live radically sold out to finishing the task of reaching the unreached.
3. To finish well we must develop some core convictions that will push us toward the finish line.
4. To finish well we must get beyond our spiritual arrogance and lack of discipline that keeps us from building our lives on God's Word.
5. To finish well we must get beyond our shortsightedness. There is coming a day when we will stand before our glorious King, and as we worship in his presence, we will not regret the sacrifice, hardship, pain, or suffering we might have endured to reach the unreached with the glorious gospel of his grace.

Questions to Consider

1. In light of the Great Commission and the desperate condition of the unreached, what do you need to reevaluate in your life today or in your plans for the future?
2. When it comes to missions, what are you convinced of? How do your convictions push you to keep on serving the Lord Jesus?
3. How can we help each other keep on going when it would be so much easier and more delightful to retire from direct participation in the progress of the gospel?

—Sources—

About Missions. *AM Quotes.* 2013. http://aboutmissions.org/quotes. html (accessed June 2013).

Adeney, Miriam. *Kingdom Without Borders: The Untold Story of Global Christianity.* Downers Grove, IL: InterVarsity, 2009.

Bakke, Ray, and Jon Sharpe. *Street Signs: A New Direction in Urban Ministry.* Birmingham, AL: New Hope, 2006.

Beeke, Joel R. *Living for God's Glory.* Lake Mary, FL: Reformation Trust, 2008.

Bibby, Reginal. *Mosaic Madness.* Toronto: Stoddard, 1990.

Borthwick, Paul. *Western Christians in Global Missions: What's the Role of the North American Church?* Downers Grove, IL: InterVarsity, 2012.

Bryant, David. "Beyond Loving the World." In *Perspectives on the World Christian Movement*, edited by Ralph D. Winter and Steven C. Hawthorne. Pasadena, CA: William Carey Library, 2009.

Coleman, Robert E. "The Master's Plan." In *Perspectives on the World Christian Movement*, edited by Ralph D. Winter and Steven C. Hawthorne. Pasadena, CA: William Carey Library, 2009.

Comfort, Ray. *God Has a Wonderful Plan for Your Life: The Myth of the Modern Message*. Bellflower, CA: Living Waters, 2010.

Corbett, Steve, and Brian Fikkert. *When Helping Hurts: How to Aleviate Poverty Without Hurting the Poor and Yourselves*. Chicago: Moody, 2009.

Corwin, Gary. "Doing Missions Like It's 1930?" *Evangelical Missions Quarterly*, April 2009.

Dever, Mark. *The Gospel and Personal Evangelism*. Wheaton, IL: Crossway, 2007.

Duvall, J. Scott, and J. Daniel Hays. *Grasping God's Word*, 3rd Edition. Grand Rapids, MI: Zondervan, 2012.

Edwards, Jonathan. "Sinners in the Hands of an Angry God." *ICL Net*. n.d. www.iclnet.org/pub/resources/text/history/spurgeon/web/edwards.sinners.html.

Ellis, B. Tyler. "9 Reasons Why You Should Be Ministering to International Students ... Yesterday." *faithoncampus.com*. February 2013. http://faithoncampus.com/9-reasons-why-you-should-be-ministering-to-international-studentsyesterday/.

Elmer, Duane. *Cross-Cultural Connections: Stepping Out and Fitting In Around the World*. Downers Grove, IL: IVP Academic, 2002.

———. *Cross-Cultural Servanthood: Serving the World in Christlike Humility*. Downers Grove, IL: IVP Books, 2006.

Fee, Gordon D., and Douglas Stuart. *How to Read the Bible for All Its Worth*. Grand Rapids, MI: Zondervan, 1981.

Gilbert, Greg. *What Is the Gospel?* Wheaton, IL: Crossway, 2010.

Grudem, Wayne A. *Systematic Theology: An Introduction to Biblical Doctrine*. Grand Rapids, MI: Zondervan, 1994.

Heart Cry Missionary Society. 2010. www.heartcrymissionary.com/about-us/statement-of-faith/essential-convictions.

Hickman, Claude, Steven C. Hawthorne, and Todd Ahrend. "Life on Purpose." In *Perspectives on the World Christian Movement* , edited by Ralph D. Winter and Steven C. Hawthorne. Pasadena, CA: William Carey Library, 2009.

Hoke, Steve, and Bill Taylor. "Your Journey to the Nations." In *Perspectives on the World Christian Movement*, edited by Ralph D. Winter and Steven C. Hawthorne. Pasadena, CA: William Carey Library, 2009.

Jakes, Lara. "Iraq Police Training: $200 Million Wasted on Police Development Program, Auditors Say." *Huffington Post*. July 30, 2012. www.huffingtonpost.com/2012/07/30/iraq-police-training-audit_n_1718137.html.

Joshua Project. *Status of World Evangelization*. March 2013. www.joshuaproject.net/assets/handouts/status-of-world-evangelization.pdf.

———. *Definitions: Unreached /Least-Reached*. May 2013. www.joshuaproject.net/definitinos.php.

———. *From Every Nation.* 2013. www.joshuaproject.net/assets/maps/from-every-nation-map.pdf.

———. *Signs of the Times—Great Commission Powerpoints.* June 2013. www.joshuaproject.net/great-commission-powerpoints.php.

Krishnan, Sunder. *Loving God with All You've Got.* Camp Hill, PA: Wing Spread, 2003.

Kroeker, Steve. *The Hero: How the Story of God Shapes Our Life Together.* Raleigh, NC: Lulu, 2011.

Lanier, Sarah A. *Foreign to Familiar.* Hagerstown, MD: McDougal, 2000.

Livermore, David A. *Serving with Eyes Wide Open: Doing Short Term Missions with Cultural Intelligence.* Grand Rapids, MI: Baker Books, 2006.

Livingood, Ellen. *Your Focus on the World.* Newtown, PA: Catalyst Services, 2010.

Mandryk, Jason. *Operation World.* 7th Edition. Colorado Springs, CO: Biblica, 2010.

Miley, George. "The Awesome Potential for Mission Found in Local Churches." In *Perspectives on the World Christian Movement,* edited by Ralph D. Winter and Steven C. Hawthorne. Pasadena, PA: William Carey Library, 2009.

Miller, Robert S. *Spiritual Survival Handbook for Cross-Cultural Workers.* Orlando, FL: BottomLine Media, 2011.

Mischke, Werner, ed. "Partnership Agreement Form." *Beauty of Partnership*. Mission ONE. 2013. http://cdn2.assets.sites. launchrocketship.com/a6347111-876c-4337-9f3f-9f712c3494ed/ files/26bd636b-f602-428a-8fda-bab183fe43ed/partnership_ agreement_2009_generic.pdf.

Muller, Roland. *Honor and Shame: Unlocking the Door*. Bloomington, IN: Xlibris, 2001.

Nichols, Stephen J. *The Reformation: How a Monk and a Mallet Changed the World*. Wheaton, IL: Crossway, 2007.

Osborne, Larry. *Accidental Pharisees: Avoiding Pride, Exclusivity, and the Other Dangers of Overzealous Faith*. Grand Rapids, MI: Zondervan, 2012.

Ott, Craig, and Gene Wilson. *Global Church Planting: Biblical Principles and Best Practices for Multiplication*. Grand Rapids, MI: Baker Academic, 2011.

Penner, James, Rachel Harder, Erika Anderson, Bruno Desorcy, and Rick Hiemstra. *Hemorrhaging Faith*. Foundational Research Document, Evangelical Fellowship of Canada, 2012.

Piper, John. *Receiving Children in Jesus' Name*. February 23, 1992. www.desiringgod.org/resource-library/sermons/receiving-children-in-jesus-name.

———. *Desiring God*. Sisters, OR: Multnomah, 2003.

———. "Everlasting Truth for the Joy of All People." *DesiringGod. org*. October 26, 2003. www.desiringgod.org/resource-library/ sermons/everlasting-truth-for-the-joy-of-all-peoples.

———. *Don't Waste Your Life*. Wheaton, IL: Crossway, 2007.

———. "The Legacy of Antioch: Partnering with the Church of the Global South." *DesiringGod.org*. October 25, 2009. www.desiringgod.org/resource-library/sermons/the-legacy-of-antioch.

———. *Let The Nations Be Glad!: The Supremecy of God in Missions*. Grand Rapids, MI: Baker Academic, 2010.

Piper, John, and David Mathis. *Finish the Mission: Bringing the Gospel to the Unreached and Unengaged*. Wheaton, IL: Crossway, 2012.

Platt, David. *Radical: Taking Back Your Faith From the American Dream*. Colorado Springs, CO: Multnomah Books, 2010.

Pocook, Michael, Gailyn Van Rheenen, and Douglas McConnell. *The Changing Face of World Missions*. Grand Rapids, MI: Baker Academic, 2005.

Salem, Paul and Charis Salem. "Welcoming International Students Strategically." *Evangelical Missions Quarterly*, April 2009.

Salmon, Jacqueline L. "Churches Retool Missions Trips." *Washington Post*. July 5, 2008. www.washingtonpost.com/wp-dyn/content/article/2008/07/04/AR2008070402233.html.

Schwartz, Glenn. "Two Awesome Problems." *International Journal of Frontier Missions*. Winter 2003. www.ijfm.org/PDFs_IJFM/21_1_PDFs/27_34_Schwartz.pdf.

Sproul, R. C. *Does God Control Everything?* Sanford, FL: Reformation Trust, 2012.

Standards of Exellence. "The 7 Standards." *Standards of Excellence in Short Term Mission.* 2013. www.soe.org/explore/the-7-standards/.

Sterret, T. Norton, and Richard L. Schultz. *How to Understand Your Bible.* Downers Grove, IL: InterVarsity Press, 2010.

Stott, Dan W. "Missionary Giants or Just a Giant Need for Prayer?" *Evangelical Missions Quarterly,* January 2005.

Stott, John R. W. "The Bible in World Evangelization." In *Perspectives on the World Christian Movement,* edited by Ralph D. Winter and Steven C. Hawthorne. Pasadena, CA: William Carey Library, 2009.

———. *The Message of Acts.* Downers Grove,IL: InterVarsity Press, 1990.

Sutter, K. *Keys to Church Planting Movements.* McKinleyville, CA: Asteroidea Books, 2006.

Swanson, Eric, and Sam Williams. *To Transform a City.* Grand Rapids, MI: Zondervan, 2010.

Ver Beek, Kurt Allen. "Lessons From the Sapling: Review of Quantitative Research on Short-term Missions." In *Effective Engagement in Short-Term Missions: Doing It Right!,* edited by Robert Priest. Pasadena, CA: William Carey Library, 2008.

Verwer, George. *Out of the Comfort Zone.* Grand Rapids, MI: Bethany House, 2000.

Washer, Paul. "Essential Convictions." *Heart Cry Missionary Society.* 2010. www.heartcrymissionary.com/about-us/statement-of-faith/essential-convictions.

Wright, Christopher J. H. *The Mission of God's People: A Biblical Theology of the Church's Mission.* Grand Rapids, MI: Zondervan, 2010.

Yohannan, K. P. *Come, Let's Reach the World.* Carollton, TX: GFA Books, 2004.

———. *Revolution in World Missions.* Carrollton, TX: GFA Books, 2004.

CPSIA information can be obtained at www.ICGtesting.com
Printed in the USA
LVOW11s1150040914

402299LV00001B/5/P